# THE RIGHT TO BE INDIAN

*by*
*E. Schusky*



**THE INDIAN HISTORIAN PRESS, INC.**

**AMERICAN INDIAN EDUCATIONAL PUBLISHERS**
**SAN FRANCISCO, CA.**

# Table of Contents

# Introduction

*The Right to be Indian* was published as a mimeographed study in 1965 by the Board of National Missions of the United Presbyterian Church in cooperation with the Institute of Indian Studies of the State University of South Dakota. The first edition was soon exhausted and a second edition was then issued. The American Indian Historical Society utilized this monograph effectively in its workshops for teachers held in 1966, publishing its own edition of the work. This too was soon exhausted.

Since the date of its first publication, *The Right to be Indian* has enjoyed a good response from teachers and scholars who have used it in classroom work. It has been used as source material and for supplementary reading in sociology, history, Native American studies, and anthropology courses. At the request of many teachers, therefore, The Indian Historian Press offers this monograph as the first in a series of *Classic Studies Reprints.* This educational publishing house was organized by the American Indian Historical Society in order to develop an accurate and authentic body of literature in the culture, history, lifeways, and current affairs of the Native American, for the use of the educational community.

*The Right to be Indian* is not, nor does it attempt to be, a definitive work on the subject. However, it has expressed a new trend of thought among nonIndian scholars and has encouraged Indian scholars in the pursuit of independent study in the affairs of their own people. That this is bound to continue and to become a ground-swell of literary works produced by Native American scholars, is now a certainty. A major step in this direction was taken by the Convocation of American Indian Scholars held in March, 1970, the first event of its kind in American history. Sponsored and organized by the American Indian Historical Society, the Convocation stimulated new efforts on the part of the Native scholars, leading to the beginning of an exciting and fascinating body of literature about America's original peoples.

Dr. Schusky's monograph deals with Indian affairs during the early 1960's. Today, with the opening of a new era in American history, Indian affairs are as bad if not worse than that described in his monograph. Areas in which the Native American still suffers deprivation, and is still to be found mired in the depths of economic poverty are found in every part of Indian life. Some few have escaped, or have won small victories over this condition – but at the cost of a loss of Indian identity, and the surrender of their *Right to be Indian.* Some small pockets of improvement have occurred, such as a certain degree of economic development on the Navajo reservation and the beginnings made in educational opportunity. But the facts described below reveal the true situation:

The national Indian average use of contaminated water is 74 percent. Eighty-one percent of all Indian families haul their domestic water. Eighty-three percent of Indian families have unsatisfactory and illegal methods for the disposal of excreta. The average size of Indian houses is less than two rooms, with an average household of more than 5.4 occupants. On the other hand, the nonIndian house has an average nationally of only 2.9 occupants and more than four rooms, (from a study by J.G. Jorgensen). The opening of educational opportunities for Indian youth since 1968 has resulted in relatively larger numbers entering colleges and universities, and receiving financial aid for higher education. However, the estimated figure of dropouts from these educational institutions is 80 percent as of mid-1970. The reasons for this are complex. Primarily, they have to do with the uncertainty of continued financial aid, the economic need of the family at home, the failure to adequately prepare the young Indian student for university life and university academic work. The failure of the educational system to meet the needs of the modern world and to prepare the young American for living in it, has affected the Native American student even more than others. Entering college, he finds an archaic curriculum, inadequate high-level instruction, and courses that lead him to question the practicality of expending some five years of his life in non-productive study. In courses having to do with American and world history, civics, sociology, government, he finds the history of his own people distorted, misinterpreted, degraded, (See

*Textbooks and the American Indian,* by Rupert Costo). That this is true not only among American Indian students, but among all others as well, is certainly a consideration; but we are concerned with the Native American student here, and he deserves much more than he is getting out of the academic community today.

Many educational institutions have organized Native American studies courses, programs, institutes, or departments, as part of the academic offering. But these are ill-conceived, full of air, having no academic goals, lacking strong scholarly content. Very soon they collapse for sheer lack of scholarly substance. There are few scholars currently working to construct curriculum and develop courses of study to correct this situation. Fully aware of the desperate condition of his people, influenced by the growing unrest in the country at large, and conscious of the value of his own heritage, the young Indian student opts to engage in the struggle for survival of his race. Often in a mistaken cause, but just as often in a cause worthy of his best efforts, he spends his talents and gambles his whole future in the struggle for the betterment of his people and the preservation of his heritage. That this energetic revivalist movement is only beginning, is a prediction that can be made with complete safety. Furthermore, that the young Indian can and will lead this movement, depends only upon the growing wisdom of the youth leaders and the emergence of new and more sophisticated leadership.

In the economic area, efforts are being made to "bring industry to the reservation," in order to improve conditions. The Bureau of Indian Affairs, in 1968, reported that 170 million dollars were grossed from agriculture on all reservations, a total of 50 million acres, in 1966. But these figures include the estimated value of all fish and game taken by Indians on their reservations, amounting to approximately 20 million dollars, and consumed by the Indians themselves. Furthermore, of the 170 million dollars, the Native Americans actually realized only 58.6 million. Sixteen million of this amount was from rents and permits to nonIndians. Thus, fully 127 and a half million, or 75 percent of the gross from agriculture, went to nonIndians. The Indians received a mere pittance for the exploitation of their own lands by non-Indians.

Efforts of the federal government to develop independent Indian resources and economy are highly touted in the mass media throughout the country. Lumbering is big business in the United States, and Indian reservations still have great stands of trees highly desirable for this industry. In 1967, about 803 million board feet of lumber was cut. Only 100 million board feet, or about 12 percent of the total, was processed in tribal sawmills. According to Jorgensen, "Indians were selling their natural resources yet maintaining practically no control over the means of production . . . As for oil and all other minerals . . . the exploitation of these resources by national and multinational corporations brought 31 millions of dollars to the tribes in 1967," but billions to the corporations. It should not be forgotten, moveover, that such funds constitute the *entire* income of many tribes, affecting thousands of families. It should also be remembered that the tribes do not have the handling of their own funds. These proceeds go to the United States Treasury, to be held *for the tribes* and administered by the Bureau of Indian Affairs, from which all sorts of administrative costs – unauthorized by the tribes – are deducted. Thus, states Jorgensen, "It is evident that the corporations are generating capital for themselves and offering Indian tribes carrots in the form of lease and royalty incomes, whereas the Indians are losing their resources." Attention should also be drawn to the fact, omitted by Jorgensen, that such leases are generally for 99 years, a guarantee for continuing Indian poverty, unemployment, and deprivation. Federal agents, in "selling" the idea for such long-term leases, argue that Indian people would be hired to form the labor force. This, while it may happen at first, is soon a lost hope, for almost without exception nonIndians become the major part of the labor force in such projects. Between 1962 and 1968, ten thousand new jobs were created through the development of industries on or near reservations. But sixty percent of these jobs have now gone to nonIndians, according to the Indian Record of October, 1968. Private corporations are using Indian capital to expand, yet using Indian labor only in a limited way, and Indians do not maintain ownership or control of these industries. Indian people hired either in administrative or controlling positions are the great exception.

Thus, Indian economy is stifled, and the corporations grow fat on the proceeds of Indian resources. Mining companies, railroads, and industrial concerns made their millions as a result of the expropriation of Indian land. Research documents exist in the hundreds bemoaning this situation, but today expropriation continues. From a previous condition of self-support, self reliance, and self-government – those conditions which constituted the *rights* of the Indian, and guaranteed him the *right to be Indian*, the Native American has been forced into underdevelopment, is now locked in poverty, moves to urban areas only to find that he has extended his condition of impoverishment, and is trapped in the web of American society's jungle of mismanagement, exploitation, and the superstructure of American big business interests. The alphabetized governmental agencies such as OEO, CAP, BIA, and so on, are only a continuation of a monstrous American welfare system, not only unsatisfactory and insufficient, but degrading to man.

It is a fact that the Bureau of Indian Affairs, the Secretary of the Interior, and the House Committee on Interior and Insular Affairs control Indian economic development. The decision-making power is in their hands, not in the hands of the Indian tribes. In certain cases, where a big hoo-rah has been raised over the granting of decision-making powers to the tribes, the facts always reveal that this is a mere showpiece. The final word is through Congressional legislation, through the Bureau of Indian Affairs hierarchy, or through the Secretary of the Interior. Traditionally, the Indian has gone to Congress for relief. That is because Congressional action is the only certain way in which to obtain remedies, due to the peculiarities of Federal-Indian relationships. However, considering that Congress is subjected to the political influence of big business and commercial interests lobbyists, that congressmen have certain political debts to pay, and that big business actually controls the decisions made by Congress, no hope can be found from that source, in the long view of Indian development.

It is no comfort to the American Indian, the first American to suffer from "under-development," to know that poor farmers, poor shopkeepers, poor farm laborers, and poor cattlemen, are now suffering from this same disease because of the huge and growing power of big business, big farm interests, and big mineral and oil interests.

*The Right to be Indian* raises some extremely vital questions for the Native American, and for American society as a whole. It raises the question of *why* Indians have the right to be different, politically as well as socially and economically. What it does not do is spell out these rights. A brief enumeration of such rights includes these:

The right to maintain and preserve what remains of our cultural heritage and our human values. The elements of this cultural heritage include but are not limited to the use and teaching of our native languages. To maintain and develop our own courts of justice in our way and not in the inhuman western way, as is now the case. Priority in educational opportunity for the First Americans, whose land this was and is today. Priority in obtaining lands in the public domain without payment for the same, since these lands are ours by original occupancy, for which no amount of dollars can repay us. The right to reclaim lands not in private use for the purposes of developing our economy in the way that we believe it is best to so develop it, without interference from governmental or other agencies. The right to choose our own experts, our own professionals, engineers and developers . . . so that they shall be responsible to the Indian people and must account to the people for their work and actions. The right not to be compelled to fight a foreign war on foreign soil against a foreign people whom we do not even know. The right to so develop our economy and our lands so that our people can come home from the urban ghettos and make a life for themselves free from hunger and disease, with some hope of a better future for their children. The right to control our own school systems, select our own school boards, choose our own textbooks, hire our own teachers, approve our own curriculum and course content, and utilize our own corps of scholars.

There is a tremendous resurgence among American Indians today. This is more than the promise of a dead people and a dead past come to life once more, such as the Ghost Dance movement was. It is more than the teaching of the rules of life and living, such as the religion of Handsome Lake was. It is a revivalist movement combining the best of the old and the best of the new, in which youth and adult will soon find a common cause. To a land sick with the economic disease of its own making, corrupted by its greed and careless disregard for the laws of nature, this tiny population of Natives who once were the great of the land, may well hold out the promise of a better future for all.

The American Indian
Historical Society
July 1970

**(Note: A Bibliographical addenda has been added to Ernest Schusky's own bibliography and may be found at the end of the monograph. Many of the works quoted in the addenda were not available at the time of writing of the monograph.)**

chapter 1

# INDIANS IN THE CURRENT STRUGGLE FOR CIVIL RIGHTS

The problem of extending full civil rights to Indians is highly intricate. Indians were made citizens by an Act of Congress in 1924 but, because of a long and complicated history of Indian and Federal Government relations, they have many additional rights guaranteed by treaty. These rights, unfortunately, sometimes prevent enjoyment of the rights of other Americans. In the current struggle for civil rights, Indians must be singled out for special treatment if their former rights are to be protected as much as possible while they are in the process of receiving their proper place as citizens.

In addition to this complexity, Indians on reservations generally live in poverty. Low living standards are so striking that their emphasis may lead to a neglect of civil rights. Of course, economic conditions are closely linked with civil rights, and the problem of poverty must be solved. However, it should be remembered that economic improvement *alone* is far from sufficient in improving the present situation of Indians.

The magnitude of Indian poverty seems to have obscured the problem of particular rights to even a man like Hubert H. Humphrey, a long-standing advocate of civil rights and an acknowledged expert in the field. In personal correspondence (May, 1964) Humphrey writes: " . . . the Civil Rights Act protects the rights of all Americans. This protection will be of particular benefit to any group which has suffered from discrimination, and this has too often been the lot of the American Indian. Civil rights, of course, are inextricably linked to economic and educational opportunity."

Humphrey clarified his view on the importance of poverty in an address to the American Indian Capital Conference on Poverty in May, 1964.

> There is nothing new about the evils of poverty. Its destructive toll on the human spirit – even more than its social cost in welfare and disease – has torn at our sense of justice. What is new about poverty is that it is not necessary . . .
>
> The American Indian presents a special case in two important respects. First, the Federal Government is deeply involved because it has the major responsibility for Indian affairs, and is the trustee for reservations where the majority of the Indians live; and, second, Indians have special cultural problems which make it more difficult to integrate them into the economic life of a modern society with its rapid technological developments . . .
>
> The American Indian, because his cultural problems are so difficult, provides a more critical laboratory in which to learn to deal with these problems. Indian reservations can become excellent pilot projects or models of what can be done – and how to do it – in the war on poverty.

A similar view is officially expressed by the Bureau of Indian Affairs. Mr. Leonard Ware, Chief of Correspondence and Reports, writes in May, 1964, that:

> We should like to point out that so far as Indians today may suffer from unfair discrimination in education, employment or public accommodations, the President's civil rights legislative program will, if enacted, definitely help them as it will all minority groups in the country. Bureau policy and all of its programs are aimed toward the goals set forth in [The Report by the Task Force on Indian Affairs].

It is necessary to analyze this report in some detail because it appears to be the foundation of present policy. The task force, appointed by President Kennedy, consisted of: W.W. Keeler, Phileo Nash (a former Commissioner of Indian Affairs), James Officer and William Zimmerman. The group conferred with many Indians, members of Congress, Bureau officials and anthropologists. The report was concluded in mid-1961.

The bulk of the report is directed at analysis of economic problems and organization of the Bureau of Indian Affairs. Almost one-quarter of the report describes the administrative organization of the Bureau. The forty percent which describes economic development and community services is vital for planning, but relatively little attention is given to the need of Indians for protection of their rights. In the introduction, the task force notes: "The distinct legal status of Indians is a further hindrance to the abolishment of the Bureau of Indian Affairs and the withdrawal of the Federal Government from this field. In many decisions, the United States Supreme Court has upheld Washington's responsibility for helping Indians find solutions to their problems." However, the report does little to suggest how the "distinct legal status" is to be protected in the future, although a section on Federal-State relations does point up some of the special problems which Indians face.

This position differs in emphasis from that of many Indians. They are well aware of their economic problems and stress them strongly, but a comparable emphasis is laid on rights. Indians note that if these rights were protected, then economic problems would not be so great. For instance, at the American Indian Chicago Conference Indians pointed out that incomes on many reservations are threatened by disregard of treaty rights.

> Grave concern has arisen as a result of the recent rulings of the Bureau of Internal Revenue which in substance directly violate the solemn treaty obligations made with the American Indian.
>
> In fact, within the past few years, there has been a steady trend by both the federal and state taxing departments to encroach upon the rights of the Indian in the taxing of Indian property.[1]

As an example of the arbitrary position of Internal Revenue, Indians pay income tax on profits from cattle raised on trust land. They do not have to pay taxes on alfalfa raised on the same land. Indians recognize that the Internal Revenue Service is not entirely at fault; what is needed is clarifying legislation. The report of the Chicago Conference continues: "In order to further prevent the establishment of such arbitrary rules of the Bureau of Internal Revenue, and to correct the rules already existing, we deem it necessary that legislation be enacted which will clearly spell out the intent and purposes of the existing treaties and agreements made with Indian tribes."[2]

Rights linked with economic privilege were not the only concern of Indians at the Chicago Conference. A section of their report emphasized the rights provided by treaty and an expression of expectation that these rights would be respected. The far-reaching implications of these rights may be noted in just one of the paragraphs devoted to treaty rights.

> The right of self-government, a right which the Indian possessed before the coming of the white man, has never been extinguished; indeed, it has been repeatedly sustained by the courts of the United States. Our leaders made binding agreements – ceding lands as requested by the United States;

> keeping the peace; harboring no enemies of the nation. And the people stood with the leaders in accepting these obligations.[3]

The report also reminds the larger society of its obligations in respect to treaty rights. The Indians at Chicago noted what Chief Justice Marshall said of Indian treaties.

> Such a treaty . . . is a compact between two nations or communities, having the right of self-government. Is it essential that each party shall possess the same attributes of sovereignty to give force to the treaty? This will not be pretended, for, on this ground, very few valid treaties could be formed. The only requisite is, that each of the contracting parties shall possess the right of self-government and the power to perform the stipulations of the treaty.[4]

As Indians come to express their views on the Indian "problem," one sees special stress on the protection of Indian civil rights. Indians, of course, are as aware of their poverty as anyone, but they do not let economic problems obscure their quest for protection of their special rights. This position sometimes leads to contradictory stands, but emphasis on their rights is always clear. Thus, the National Congress of American Indians refrained from endorsement of the 1964 Civil Rights Act. Their position was explained by Mr. Robert Burnette, then Executive Director, in personal correspondence (April, 1964).

> We as the National Congress of American Indians have not taken a position on the Civil Rights Bill in Congress because there is fear among the Tribes that it will tend to hurt their treaty Rights.
>
> It is bad enough the Congress continues to break our treaties without just compensation as was done in the Crow Creek-Lower Brule Case where land was taken by an Act of Congress and the Indians were paid nine years later without any consideration for interest that should have been applied when paid.
>
> My opinion of what can be done on Civil Rights violations among Indian people is very simple, for all the United States Government needs to do is to carry out the law irregardless of what the law was in integration cases. This also applies to Indian cases, but, because we lack the political strength, Indians are ignored and their rights are therefore trampled upon by the very people who are being enriched by our property. The United States District Attorneys have not carried out their responsibilities towards Indians and the guaranteed guardianship of the United States government has completely fallen apart since 1953.

An organization of Indian youth took a quite different stand on the legislation, but they, too, pointed up the need for special recognition of rights. The following excerpts are from a letter prepared for Senator Humphrey. (The letter was later revised; only the original was available to the author.)

> The National Indian Youth Council is shocked and dismayed to hear that the National Congress of American Indians, at a most crucial time, has declined to take a stand on the current Civil Rights legislation . . .
>
> The NIYC would like to go on record as unqualifiedly supporting and endorsing the Civil Rights Bill. Further, we feel it necessary to say at this time that the National Congress of American Indians' action does not represent the opinion of most American Indians . . .
>
> Civil Rights legislation will certainly be a boon to Indians who live in those states which socially and legally discriminate against them. The vicious discrimination practiced in areas bordering Indian country must be stopped . . . Legal chicanery to immobilize the Indian vote in many states is comparable to the Negro situation in Mississippi. This is only part of the vicious discrimination that the Civil Rights legislation will alleviate for Indians.

But a final solution, according to the NIYC, would require more than the present legislation.

> Segregation and exploitation is enough of a cross to bear, but the Indian is attacked in his own home and community. Even the educational system on reservations, over which Indians have no control, is explicitly aimed at breaking up his family and community. Further, what few rights by treaty an Indian has left to him – the last sign that he might be able to survive as a people – are being eroded away by high-handed action on the part of state governments and, unwittingly we believe, by unilateral action on the part of Congress.
>
> This system under which Indians live, which is a horrendous combination of colonialism, segregation and discrimination, has been going on for over 100 years. The result is that Indians are not only uneducated and poverty-stricken, helpless and without hope, divided among themselves, but also confused and threatened beyond belief. There must be some drastic steps in the way of legislation to accompany the present Civil Rights legislation in order to remedy this 100 years of intolerable and destructive discrimination.

The recommendations of the NIYC give a general indication of what would be required to fully protect Indian rights.

> (1) The decision-making power in Indian communities must be put back where it belongs, in the hands of the people and the community . . . This does not mean that we are advocating that Indians must be thrown under state control. Indians cannot afford to pay taxes on their land; they just do not have the money, and, if they were to lose their resources, the job of economic rehabilitation will be just that much harder. At the present time, given the inexperienced state in which Indians find themselves and the climate of sentiment in states with large Indian populations, state control over Indian affairs could only mean that Indians would be shorn of their resources.
>
> (2) Indian tribes are not large and powerful politically, but we do not feel that this then gives state governments or the federal government the right

> to disregard and violate existent treaties . . . *Indian consent,* not "consultation", is needed in any drastic restructuring of the relationship, spelled out in treaties, between the federal government and Indian tribes.
>
> (3) A drastic and revolutionary economic and education program must be undertaken in Indian communities to overcome this 100 years of vicious discrimination which has resulted in the present condition of Indians.

Support or non-support of civil rights legislation is only a tactical difference among Indians. Both the NCAI and the NIYC recognize that their rights differ from other minority groups and particular legislation is needed to secure these rights. In short, Indian rights are not now protected fully; Indians are in a unique position and their classification with other minority groups is to their disadvantage. The goal of many Indians is to maintain a separate culture and community, whereas they believe other minorities hope for integration and assimilation. This view is well expressed by Sandra Johnson.[5]

> Since the public's attention is being turned toward civil rights, many people are equating the struggle of the American Indian with that of the American Negro. Actually, their situations are almost exactly opposite. The Negroes are striving to attain assimilation with the dominant white society, while the Indians are striving to resist this forced assimilation with the rest of society.
>
> The Negro at the present time, unlike the Indians, has nothing to preserve in the way of land, culture, language or traditional arts and crafts. He is an uprooted people who is concentrating his struggle in legal rights. The Indians already have full citizenship rights and so their legal struggle is to retain rather than attain . . .
>
> Everywhere, lip service has been given by churchmen and government officials alike that the great Indian heritage ought to be preserved. And everywhere, there is the same support of measures which lead to the destruction of Indian culture. All the educational relocation bills have been aimed at getting the Indian off the reservation and into the city . . . . Are we willing to protect and promote individual rights when they are not similar to our own? The answer seems to be "no".

The Indian stand in the current struggle for civil rights may not always be clear, but two important points do appear. First, the poverty of Indians is so overriding that it sometimes obscures the need for protection of Indian rights. Generally, the dominant society tends to emphasize the economic problems to the detriment of rights. It is easy to believe that, given economic opportunity and general civil rights legislation, the Indian "problem" will disappear. Indians, on the other hand, see the need for clarification of their rights as special citizens. Certainly, they too recognize their dire economic straits, but improvement in this area alone is not enough.

The argument that Indians are "special" citizens and, therefore, deserve special rights may at first appear to run counter to the American value of equality. However, these rights would not make Indians unequal; they would simply allow them to be different. It must be emphasized that these rights are not due Indians because of their race or birth; the peculiar legal status of Indians is a matter of contract or consent. Felix Cohen has well summarized this argument.

> The special rights of the Indians are like the rights of other groups that have special claims upon the Federal Government, for example, homesteaders, or veterans, or holders of Federal securities, or government employees, or government contractors. Each of these groups has special rights, because of service performed, and incidental to these special rights are certain special disabilities. A homesteader may not alienate his homestead. A government employee may not prosecute claims against the government, which is the right of any other citizen. A government contractor may not hire and fire as he pleases or work his employees more than a certain number of hours. These disabilities are not forms of discrimination against oppressed groups, but simply necessary safeguards incidental to the process of securing special benefits or payments from the Federal Government. By and large, it must be remembered, whatever we have given to Indians and whatever we give them today is not a matter of charity, but is a part of a series of real estate transactions through which about 90 percent of the land of the United States was purchased from the Indian by the Federal Government.[6]

In the "real estate transactions" a fantastically complex relationship between the Federal Government and Indians developed. On the one hand, treaties, Acts of Congress and Supreme Court decisions came to play a part in the definition of Indian, Indian reservations and Indian rights. These definitions are explored in Chapter II. In addition to legislative and judicial policy, the executive branch developed plans for Indians which involved far more than acquisition of land. Various philosophies about what "should be done" for Indians have led to the present day, intricate legal status of the first Americans. Chapter III is an introduction to this history which makes Indians special citizens.

chapter 2

# THE BACKGROUND

I. **Who is an Indian?** It is important to recognize who is an Indian for two purposes. First, many Indians and whites have assumed that Indians are rapidly disappearing and that, once they are gone, there will no longer be an "Indian problem." Of course, it could be argued that eventual disappearance does not justify any disregard for the civil rights of the present population, but it will be shown below that the idea of a "vanishing Indian" is only a myth. Second, a definition of *Indian* is needed for an understanding of the situation. Differences among definitions of who is an Indian contribute much to the legal and social problems facing Indians today.

A. **Are Indians Disappearing?** Initial confusion over the question of who is an Indian arose because of data collection by the U.S. Bureau of the Census and the Bureau of Indian Affairs. The Bureau of the Census reports as an Indian any "person of mixed white and Indian blood . . . if enrolled in an Indian agency or reservation roll, or if not so enrolled, if the proportion of Indian blood is one-fourth or more, or if the person is regarded as an Indian in the community where he lives." Actually, census takers have in the past determined race by inspection and may omit specific questions about race. Therefore, a number of enrolled Indians living off the reservation or Indians of more than one-quarter blood must be inaccurately reported.

The Bureau of the Census figures for the Indian population are also misleading because of occasional special censuses. In 1910 and 1930 unusual efforts were made to enumerate Indians. As a result, persons were counted as "Indian" in 1930 who were recorded otherwise in 1920. In short, the census counts cannot be relied upon to give an accurate picture of what is happening to the Indian population.

The Bureau of Indian Affairs compiles its own population figures, but these are primarily for legal purposes. Records must be kept of Indians eligible for enrollment in the tribe. These records are suitable for the purposes of the Bureau but, unfortunately, no standard definitions of "Indian" have been devised. As a result, Bureau figures are also unreliable for demographic analysis of the Indian population. In recent years the Bureau has shown a greater interest in the problem of accurate and standard reporting. Much more complete records are being compiled, and the data are being made available through the use of punch card tabulations. However, a number of problems still plague the Bureau in population analysis. **(See Note 1.)**

Working with the available figures, J. Nixon Hadley[7] presents the evidence which should destroy the myth of "The Vanishing American." He reports that the various, reliable estimates of the aboriginal population agree on a figure of less than a million. This population did decline rapidly until 1850 when there were only about 250,000. However, for a number of reasons, the Indian population held constant for about fifty years and then began increasing. From 1900 to 1950 the number of Indians increased to over 400,000. Rapidly decreasing death rates account for most of this increase, but Indian birth rates are also high. Hadley assumes that death rates will continue to drop without an immediate corresponding decrease in the birth rate. Using conservative estimates, the Indian population projected to 1975 will be about 720,000 for the United States. The increase represents a growth rate of over fifty percent in comparison with an overall growth rate for the United States of less than forty percent.

It should be remembered that Hadley's estimate of future population rests largely on estimates from Census or Bureau figures. If these figures were low and his estimation on the conservative side, then the Indian population of the 1970's could well reach the million mark. A well-reasoned argument has already been made that the available figures on the Indian population are low. In the late 1950's Sol Tax[8] expressed dissatisfaction with the definitions and enumeration of American Indians. With two other anthropologists and a number of contributions, he began his own analysis of the Indian population. Results show the Indian population may be considerably higher than was suspected. The anthropologists counted Indians on Bureau rolls and those Indians who live in an Indian community and define themselves as Indians.

Their definition was still restrictive and they point up several omissions. Their total for 1950 was an Indian population of 434,000. This figure compares with a Census count for 1950 of 343,410 and an Indian Bureau figure of 402,286. In a later revision of their figures, the anthropologists, adding some previously omitted communities, arrived at 571,784 as the Indian population for 1950. **(See Note 2.)**

B. **How to Define "Indian."** The discrepancies in estimates of population may be accounted for largely on the basis of differences in definition of who is an Indian. The differences between the Census Bureau and Bureau of Indian Affairs have been noted. Professor Tax and his associates developed a definition of "societal" Indian with a focus on individuals who lived in Indian communities and identified themselves as Indians. It follows that such people must also have some kind of Indian culture. And it is precisely cultural differences which make some civil rights problems of Indians unique. The description and analysis of this situation must come later, but the relevance of Tax's figures should be noted here. It may also be noted that Tax is not alone in his definition. Louisa Shotwell[9] after reviewing a number of definitions, concludes, "Probably the most reasonable working definition for us is this: An Indian is somebody of Indian descent who continues to think of himself as an Indian and whom the community thinks of as Indian . . ."

Indians are often considered "wards" of the government. The concept of wardship is generally traced to a Supreme Court case in which Chief Justice Marshall ruled that an Indian tribe was not a foreign nation, but rather a domestic, dependent nation. He further interpreted that the position of a tribe *resembles* that of a ward to a guardian. Resemblance, of course, does not make a tribe a ward; certainly it does not mean that individual Indians are wards of the government. However, wardship soon became a popular word for describing the relationship between Indians and the federal government. Many Indian agents and even Congressmen justified acts on this basis. Many violations of civil and political rights occurred because "ward" became part of the meaning of Indian. Religious practices, marriage and inheritance rules, rights to land and resources were all trampled on the justification that the Indian was a ward of the government. Despite the fact that in the early 1900's an Act of Congress specifically made all Indians United States citizens, confusion remains. To understand why the idea of "ward" is so persistent, it is necessary to understand the nature of Indian reservations.

II. **What is an Indian Reservation?** Indian reservations, on occasion, have been called "concentration camps." Such a label is generally much resented by Indians and is unfair to government officials who developed the policy of locating Indians on reservations. The "development" of a reservation "policy" is misleading. Like Topsy, the idea of reservations seems to have just "growed." Under President Andrew Jackson the United States planned to move Indians in the East west of the Mississippi. However, some states such as New York reserved areas for Indians and allowed them to remain in their home territories. Further, the present state of Oklahoma, known then as Indian Territory, came to be the locale of Indian settlement. Although Indian Territory placed territorial limits on Indians, there was little governmental influence on the tribes. With westward expansion, other Indian areas were created, especially in the Northern Plains. Treaty after treaty reduced these areas and, as economic resources such as the buffalo disappeared, the government began to manage more and more of Indian life.

Before anyone was clearly aware of the consequences, Indians were living a segregated life on what became known as reservations. Segregation seems an appropriate generalization for reservation life because Indians were interdependent upon the larger society and yet not allowed full participation in that society. On the other hand, there were strict rules about not leaving the reservation, and many Indians had no desire to do so. They clung to traditional ways as much as possible. The idea that Indians were wards, coupled with almost complete economic dependence, made it possible for an Indian agent to assume dictatorial powers. Still, the reservation was land owned by a tribal group and supposedly under tribal jurisdiction.

The nature of the reservation changed greatly in the late 1800's. First, the former patterns of social control broke down in a number of tribes. Former Indian leaders were deprived of their power, traditional supports of the norms, such as religion, were weakened, or new conditions simply could not be met by traditional ways. As a result, the federal government assumed jurisdiction over some crimes and informally agents took on more power. More importantly, a movement for assimilation of Indians reached a peak, and Senator Dawes introduced legislation in 1887 which would deliberately break up the reservation system. The Senator's bill, popularly known as "Allotment," has had such far-reaching consequences that it must be thoroughly understood.

The Allotment Act arose in the agrarian era. The West was being settled by homesteaders who received a quarter section of land. What could be more fair than to allot Indians a quarter section of land and train them to be farmers? The homesteading life was a kind of ideal (except, perhaps, to many of the luckless homesteaders); most Indians were subsisting on rations doled out by the government and, in view of the Protestant ethic, souls could be saved by hard work; finally, of course, federal funds could be saved if Indians became self-supporting. In fairness, Dawes and many organized groups in the East, must be given credit for acting with the best of intentions. In the West, a number of politicians quickly joined the allotment forces because they saw the policy would open more land to settlement.

Allotment was generous in that it generally provided a quarter section of land to each Indian. Thus, an Indian family of four received a section of land, while a homesteading family of comparable size settled on a quarter section. Even so, many reservations had excess land after allotment; it was opened to homesteaders. In fact, the reservations were often checkerboarded with white settlers interspersed among Indians to set an example.

Of course, "uncivilized Indians" could not be expected to become fully assimilated in a few years. The land assigned to them was to be held *in trust* by the U.S. government for twenty-five years. In the trust period Indians could not sell their property without consent; neither did they have to pay taxes. The "trust" status of land led to numerous unforeseen consequences. One, the states could or would not provide such services as education or law to people they could not tax. The Bureau, therefore, continued such services. Two, who was to assume jurisdiction over such land? The matter was solved by continuing the former practices, except where individuals ended the trust status and enjoyed full title to their property. At this point they became taxpaying citizens; their land, and jurisdiction over it, was regarded as comparable to other state citizens, such as the whites who had settled within reservation boundaries. In short, the reservation was now fragmented into: a) white-owned tracts, b) Indian-owned tracts with title comparable to whites, and c) Indian-owned land in trust status. The states assumed jurisdiction over a and b; the tribe and federal government retained control over c. Finally, allotment created a fantastic problem of land ownership. Most allotments were not terminated at the end of twenty-five years, and the trust land began to be inherited by numerous heirs. This land, known today as "heirship land," causes an endless amount of bookkeeping. A description of the problems of heirship lands must be reserved for later discussion.

It is necessary at this point to summarize the nature of the reservation by the early 1900's. During the 1800's Indian territories had been more and more carefully delineated. They also gradually diminished in size. Initially, Indians had been totally responsible for their own affairs as long as they left whites alone. As their economic base collapsed, the federal government exerted greater control, and Congress authorized federal jurisdiction formally over major crimes. With allotment, further land was lost, individual Indian property rights were meant to replace tribal rights, and states assumed jurisdiction over certain tracts of land within reservation boundaries. The situation was such that if a crime were committed, it might be prosecuted by the state or the tribe, depending upon which side of a road the act had occurred. It is conceivable that an act might be considered a crime on one acre but not the next; it was a matter of course that the procedure and punishment for a crime differed between state and tribe.

This state of affairs was far from the American tradition, but no real attempt to solve the problem was initiated until the 1930's. Then an extensive overhaul of Indian relations was made; indeed, an entirely new policy was conceived. Known as the Indian Reorganization Act, the new policy was largely the product of Franklin Roosevelt's Commissioner of Indian Affairs, John Collier. The Indian Reorganization Act, or IRA, had many objectives. Its primary aims were to make Indians self-governing and to improve economic conditions. Model constitutions and law codes were devised by the Bureau; the tribes adapted or modified them as they wished. For the first time in United States history the Indians had a choice in policy. On most reservations tribal councils were organized which were to operate in a way comparable to city or county councils. In economic development, the trust status of land was officially continued. (During the 1920's, when the trust period had expired for many allotments, it was unofficially continued.) Furthermore, a revolving loan fund was established. Tribes could borrow with low interest rates for investments such as land and cattle. Land purchased by the tribe went into trust. Many tribes spent much money consolidating lands which had been fragmented by allotment. On many of the Plains reservations ranching, rather than farming, was the only feasible operation; consolidating was essential for this type of development.

During the 1930's some reservations actually saw economic gains while the country as a whole was experiencing a depression, but these "gains," were from the poverty of the 1920's. However, the important part of IRA, for understanding Indian civil rights, is that some reservation lands reverted to *tribal* ownership and this ownership was in *trust.* Again, the trust status was enacted for the best interests of Indians, and Indians were glad to enjoy the privilege. Not only was tax relief provided by the measure, but further federal aid and protection were built into the system.

Yet, no one fully understood that the trust status of tribal lands would prohibit true self-government. The major part of tribal business, carried on by democratically elected councils, was concerned with tribal property. (In addition to land, other investments such as cattle, sometimes "enjoyed" trust protection.) Property in the trust status was ultimately the responsibility of the Secretary of the Interior, or, in fact, the Bureau of Indian Affairs. Decisions on expenditures of funds were made by tribal councils but, where such decisions seemed "unwise," they were subject to veto by the Bureau. The Bureau found itself in the unenviable position of attempting to delegate *authority* to tribal councils while it remained *responsible* for most tribal affairs. The dilemma may be illustrated by actual example. Bureau officials on the Menomini Reservation allowed the tribe to manage its own forest with a minimum of supervision. During a period of mismanagement the tribe lost a considerable sum of money. The tribe then successfully sued the Bureau of Indian Affairs for allowing the mismanagement.

It is obvious that no bureaucrat, regardless of his intentions, can allow a tribal council to make plans which he deems unwise. In short, the tribal governments do not have final responsibility, and most Indians have become fully aware of this fact. As a result, Indians are apathetic about their local government, and tribal council officers are frequently without influence in their communities. Indeed, given the situation, it is surprising so many energetic and forceful leaders do serve on tribal councils. Under the circumstances, these leaders often appear to turn elsewhere to express their leadership. Unfortunately, there are not sufficient data to support the obvious conclusion: when forceful leaders are frustrated as tribal chairmen, they find new ways to express their talents.

Another aspect of the IRA was cultural pluralism. Indians were expected to develop their own talents and to govern themselves as much as possible in their own ways. Not only were Indians expected to profit, but American society would be richer with a diversity of ways. The value of heterogeneity *vs.* homogeneity or cultural pluralism *vs.* assimilation has been much debated in America. It appears that there are highly ambivalent feelings toward the issue.

It is not surprising, then, that Indian policy changed once again. In 1948 the direction of the IRA came to an end. (It should be noted that during the Second World War the Indian Bureau suffered from lack of funds and personnel; it did not pursue its policy vigorously from 1941 to 1945.) President Truman appointed a Commissioner of Indian Affairs who was expected to end the Bureau of Indian Affairs. Later, Congress passed a resolution which emphasized that the full rights of citizenship should be brought home to Indians; however, the resolution also set the scene for legislation which would end the federal relationship with Indians. Soon, some reservations were scheduled to have their status *as reservations* terminated. Also some obligations of the Bureau were transferred to other agencies. For instance, the Public Health Service took over the health facilities formerly provided by the Bureau, and states were encouraged to assume more responsibility for education.

Much opposition to the new policy quickly developed. Termination was seen by many Indians as threatening, and opposition to it united them within and between reservations. Indian lobbying groups, such as the National Congress of American Indians, assumed new significance, and the value of a distinct way of life on reservations became more and more conscious to Indians themselves. In short, the nature of the reservation under termination policy was changed on minor technical points such as the introduction of the Public Health Service as a new agency. It was changed to a much greater degree because an Indian way of life was greatly threatened, and Indians became much more aware of the values represented by the reservation.

In 1960, termination policy came to a standstill. President Kennedy appointed a special task force to study the Indian problem. He probably foresaw the development of a comprehensive plan which would give Indians the benefits of full citizenship yet allow an Indian way of life. This aim would probably be approved by most people, but the means for reaching this end are not at all clear. The task force, one of whose members was Phileo Nash, an anthropologist, spent much time in investigation. Nash was later appointed Commissioner of Indian Affairs. He has not yet introduced any comprehensive legislation to Congress which might indicate the goals of the present administration. He has worked hard to improve economic conditions on reservations, the most immediate and pressing problem of Indians. Improvements can be seen, but it should be noted that even termination policy called for economic development of the reservations. The poverty of Indians is so great it could not be ignored under any kind of policy; it would be unworthy of American tradition, however, if economic problems were to obscure the numerous other problems of Indians, especially of civil rights.

III. **Summary: Indians and Civil Rights.** The definition of "Indian" is closely linked with the nature of reservations, and the meaning of "Indian" is tied to civil rights. Although an Act of Congress gave full citizenship to Indians, most Indian property is in a special relation to the federal government, and the trust status actually does make the Indian a special kind of citizen. Probably the greatest restriction on this special citizen is his lack of meaningful participation or voice in local government. It is precisely at this level that some self-control is essential because of the strong desire to insure and perpetuate a distinct way of life. The matter is so important that a later chapter will be devoted to it.

In addition to the restrictions on self-government, reservation life also creates some unique situations. On the one hand, a school operated by the Bureau prohibits any local control. All school employees are civil servants and responsible to the Bureau. Indians have no formal control, whatsoever, over the education of their children. On the other hand, as citizens, they enjoy the franchise in every state and can vote for state as well as national officials. This privilege means that Indians can participate in the election of officials, from the county sheriff to the governor, who may have no jurisdiction over them. The situation has been described jokingly as "representation without taxation."

The matter, of course, is far from a joke. The situation often creates hard feelings between Indians and whites and is only one of numerous problems which makes difficulties for the "special" citizen. Before analyzing these problems further, it will be necessary to review further some historical developments in regard to Indians. The definition of Indian and the nature of the reservation underlie and are further complicated by treaty rights, Supreme Court decisions, and the understandings or misunderstandings which have developed between Indians and other citizens.

chapter 3

# WHY INDIANS ARE SPECIAL CITIZENS

The preceding chapter introduced the thesis that Indians are a special kind of citizen and as such will require legislation and aid beyond that of other minority groups. The idea is further documented in this chapter, and other aspects of Indian history are explored in order to show the peculiar nature of Indians as citizens. The status of Indians, *as different*, often becomes painfully clear in Congressional hearings. Not only is it obvious that communication between whites and Indians is exceedingly difficult but, also, a further barrier is the complexity of the Indian situation which is often almost beyond comprehension. Testimony gathered before a Senate subcommittee illustrates the point. An Indian, Mr. Cequala, is complaining of treatment he has received from the Indian agent, Mr. Jermark.

William Cequala, sworn to testify to the truth, the whole truth, and nothing but the truth, testified as follows; Mr. Dillon acted as interpreter:

> Mr. Cequala: I want to ask first, when you came here, did Mr. Jermark go to meet you?
>
> Senator Frazier: No; we went to the agency when we came here.
>
> Mr. Cequala: And he did not go to meet you?
>
> Senator Frazier: No.

By Senator Frazier:

Q. Have you had any trouble with the agent – what happened on October 26, 1926?

A. I was insulted in the agent's office, Mr. Jermark's office. He came out, and I said hello to him and went inside the office, and he said you come here and you are mad, and I said yes; and he said I have got this, and he pulled out a great big drawer and show me a gun there and a billy. I want to tell that man that you come here to investigate things like this so you never do any good and I am afraid of you as I listen you was going to put this through, and, my friend, you ought to take your agent home; if he was here I would say so; if he was here I would have taken him, or would you leave him and go on home. Now he is here, and when I tell it I see he is gone. The gun was about that long, and he show it to me and a billy. I am not drunk, but I was going to put him out. They made a law that whoever agent he was here he would not have a gun.

By Senator Wheeler:

Q. You are wrong about that?

A. That meant to that from 1868 they were not to have even pocket-knife.

Q. You were wrong about that?

A. And if they are going to have gun and keep on killing us, that is pretty bad.[10]

This situation, even for 1926, was indeed "pretty bad." To many Indians the local Indian agent was seen as a powerful tyrant holding life and death powers. Agents, of course, were not that powerful, and it is doubtful that many of them assumed the authority that could have been theirs given the Indian view of them.

However, the agent, through the B.I.A., did have extraordinary power over U.S. citizens – who happened to be Indians. The structure, which had grown piecemeal, made it impossible for Indians to enjoy fully the civil rights which they were supposed to have as citizens. It is ironical, but the events which led to deprivation of rights often involved people who thought well of Indians and attempted to see that they were given full justice.

I. **Supreme Court Decisions.** For example, one of the earliest Supreme Court cases involving Indians led to the notion that Indians were wards of the government. This case is worth examining in detail because it also emphasizes the special needs of Indian citizens.

The case derives from an act of Georgia in the 1830's when the state arbitrarily extended its jurisdiction over the Cherokee Nation. Most of the Cherokee lived within the Georgia boundaries, and they suddenly found themselves under state law. They argued that their treaties with the federal government allowed them full self-government. Moreover, state law would annihilate the Cherokee as a political society. The dispute became known as "The Case of the Cherokee Nation *vs.* the State of Georgia." The opinion of the Court, delivered by Chief Justice John Marshall, became a hallmark in defining the status of Indian tribes.

Marshall first examined the evidence for the Court's jurisdiction. The Cherokees had sued on the basis of being a foreign state, and Marshall concluded:

> So much of the argument as was intended to prove the Cherokees as a state, as a distinct political society, separated from others, capable of managing its own affairs and governing itself, has, in the opinion of a majority of the judges, been completely successful. They have been uniformly treated as a state from the settlement of our country.

However, Marshall could not agree with an argument of the plaintiff that the Cherokee constituted a foreign state in the sense of the Constitution. He admitted to an imposing argument for being foreign, but qualified the status of the Indian nations in this way:

> The condition of the Indians in relation to the United States is perhaps unlike that of any other two people in existence. In the general, nations not owning a common allegiance are foreign to each other. The term foreign nation is, with strict propriety, applicable by either to the other, but the relation of the Indians to the United States is marked by peculiar and cardinal distinctions which exist nowhere else.

It is unfortunate that this aspect of the case has not received widespread attention. It points up the unique position in which Indians find themselves. The part of the case which did become so important soon followed.

> Though the Indians are acknowledged to have an unquestionable, and, heretofore, unquestioned right to the lands they occupy, until that right be extinguished by a voluntary cession to our government; yet it may well be doubted whether those tribes which reside within the acknowledged boundaries of the United States can, with strict accuracy, be denominated foreign nations. They may, more correctly, be denominated domestic dependent nations. They occupy a territory to which we assent a title independent of their will, which must take effect in point of possession when their right of possession ceases. Meanwhile, they are in a state of pupilage. Their relation to the United States resembles that of a ward to his guardian.

The Cherokee *vs.* Georgia case is only one of the Supreme Court decisions which have placed Indians in a peculiar position as citizens. This case is of particular importance because of its reference to the relationship between the government and the tribes. Other Supreme Court decisions must also be considered in determining the rights to which Indians are entitled. Many of the Supreme Court cases are, of course, interpretations of rights granted by treaties or Acts of Congress.

II. **Treaties and Acts of Congress.** The thousands of agreements made between Indians and the Federal Government have not yet been sufficiently analyzed in detail. Here, only a brief description of this phase of Indian rights can be treated and some examples given to illustrate the special status of Indians.

In Revolutionary times, some Indian tribes were in such an important position that they could determine the course of U.S. History. The Iroquois *Nation* (a term applied by non-Indians) could have played a decisive role in 1776; a good argument could be made that if the Iroquois had sided with the British the colonies could not have won independence when they did. The Iroquois had been a most important factor in the French and Indian War, and the incipient Americans readily recognized the importance of allying or neutralizing the Iroquois. That the Iroquois remained neutral, for the most part, was most appreciated, and the early treaties with them are clearly comparable to those made with other foreign powers. Similar treaties were made with the Southeastern Indians in the War of 1812. Again, Indians were decisive in the outcome of that war. Rights granted in those treaties, as well as later ones, still must be recognized by the U.S. government. (And today some Iroquois still receive several yards of calico each year because it was promised them in an early treaty. The Iroquois demand payment in calico to emphasize the continuing validity of the treaty.) Of course, the government can break a treaty as well as make one; again, among the Iroquois the government was forced to do just this when it recently took land to build a dam. Yet, until the government admits to breaking a treaty, such rights belong to Indians.

Treaties continued to be made with Indian tribes until after the Civil War, although Marshall's decision that the tribes were a special kind of nation changed the nature of these treaties. Furthermore, in the latter part of the 19th Century negotiations with the tribes became important political matters. The House of Representatives, particularly, was concerned about their lack of participation since only the Senate must be consulted in ratification of a treaty.

Therefore, Congress passed legislation which specified that agreements with Indians would no longer be by treaty but by Acts of Congress. It would be difficult to determine if there were more or less chicanery in the Acts or treaties, but the point is unimportant here. The change in dealing with Indians still keeps them in a special relationship with the federal government. Rights provided by Acts of Congress are just as valid as treaty rights.

At this point, morality as well as legality could be questioned. Technically, an Act of Congress supersedes and is different from a treaty. Therefore, the following case may be legal but is obviously of doubtful morality. In a *treaty* with the Sioux it was stipulated that any future treaty would have to be approved by three-quarters of the adult males of the tribe. It is easy to imagine that some wise chief or leaders conceived of this stipulation in order to end any further treaty-making. Given the conditions, obtaining three-quarters of the adult males' consent to anything was most unlikely. It is hard to understand how the government representatives ever allowed such a proposition if they had any hope for future negotiations.

Soon afterward, gold was discovered in the Black Hills, and the government sought to secure this land which belonged to the Sioux by *treaty rights.* Clearly, it would have been impossible to obtain the necessary consent, but the government no longer made treaties with the Indians. Acts of Congress were now the means of negotiation, and nothing stipulated that three-quarters of the adult males would have to consent to an Act of Congress. The Black Hills were secured with a few Indian signatures agreeing to an *Act of Congress*. Some Sioux still cling to the hope of compensation for this injustice, but the value of the Black Hills is probably worth more than the national conscience.

Another interesting example of how Indian rights must be regarded may be found in a 1924 Act which confirmed citizenship on all Indians. Since the question, "Are Indians citizens?" is still common, the provision of this Act must be spelled out. The Act provided: "That all noncitizen Indians born within the territorial limits of the United States be, and are hereby, declared to be citizens of the United States, that the granting of such citizenship shall not in any manner impair or otherwise affect the right of an Indian to tribal or other property." This Act, like much government policy, was unilateral. Many Indians did want citizenship, of course, but others did not. Again, an important moral question is raised. By what right was citizenship imposed? Even today, a number of Indians refuse to recognize that they are U.S. citizens, which leads to comic-tragedy events such as the Iroquois debating whether they would declare war on Germany in 1941. The matter was settled when they decided it would be unnecessary because they had never concluded the war they had declared in 1917.[11]

III. **Indian Policy and the Bureau of Indian Affairs.** Perhaps the government's Indian policy is the best indication of why Indians are a particular kind of citizen. Some discussion of this policy was necessary in the preceding chapter; here only a general outline will be given to support the hypothesis that Indians have unique rights.

In the colonial period no overall policy toward Indians existed, and treatment of Indians varied widely. Some tribes were treated with kindness and justice. William Penn's dealings with Indians is a notable example. On the other hand, some tribes were wiped out mercilessly. Modern Indians have a telling joke. "The Puritans landed and fell on their knees to give thanks. Then they fell on the Indians."

In writing the Constitution, the founding fathers established a vague foundation for treatment of Indians. "The Congress shall have the power . . . to regulate commerce with foreign nations, and among the several states, and with the Indian Tribes." As shown previously, a policy of treaty-making and a concept of Indians as a foreign nation followed through the early 1800's.

Under President Andrew Jackson the Indian "problem" became most involved. Settlement in the Southeast was expanding, and lands of the Five Civilized Tribes were coveted. Jackson developed what became known as "Removal Policy." Indian land east of the Mississippi was to be exchanged for land in the West. Indian rights in the period developed out of Presidential actions and influence as well as Supreme Court decisions. One of the first events was the murder of a white man by an Indian on Indian land. Georgia sentenced the Indian to death; the Supreme Court ruled that Georgia lacked jurisdiction; Georgia executed the Indian anyway. There is strong indication that the execution had the tacit approval of Jackson. John Quincy Adams, in criticising Jackson's behavior in the case, charged, "The Constitution (is) prostrate in the State of Georgia . . . because the Executive of the United States is in league with the State of Georgia."

The grounds for this charge soon became even more evident. Jackson appointed a Mr. Worcester as postmaster in Cherokee country. (Worcester was also a missionary.) Worcester refused to recognize Georgia's jurisdiction by refusing to take a state license or oath as required by state law. In an appeal to the Supreme Court, Worcester *vs.* Georgia, John Marshall ruled the Georgia statutes as unconstitutional. He said, "treaties and laws of the U.S. contemplate the Indian territory as completely separate from that of the states." However, Jackson refused to enforce the Supreme Court decision, and his remark, although not documented, became famous: "John Marshall has made his decision – now let him enforce it."

These events are explained more fully by Richard Longaker.[12] His analysis of Jackson's position is most revealing. He notes that Jackson held that the Constitution did not prevent states extending authority over Indians whenever they extended their boundaries. Longaker sees this as a "feeble rationalization"; Jackson's stand was in reality based on a distaste for Marshall, a commitment to Removal Policy and a lack of sympathy for Indians. Longaker concludes that Jackson "had respect for Indian rights so long as they were exercised on the western bank of the Mississippi.[13] It may be distasteful for Americans to realize that Indian rights were so often at the discretion of the President; yet that fact is not only obvious in Jackson's administration but in many succeeding ones.

The seeds of reservation policy were contained in Removal. After Jackson, one can see the idea of delimited Indian areas growing. During the Civil War Indians were ignored except where they could be used in the struggle. But shortly after 1865 the notion of a continent filling with states was seen. That there was little concern for Indian rights during this period may be partially excused because of a strong belief that Indians would soon disappear. Indeed, their population had decreased at a rapid rate as noted before. It may also be recalled that during this period the rights of Indians frequently came completely under the jurisdiction of a local agent, generally a patronage appointment and far too often a man susceptible to easy graft. It would be difficult for Indians to claim any special rights granted during this period; there were none.

However, the national conscience became stirred late in the 19th Century and the Indian "question" again became a lively issue. Easterners for the most part saw Indians as worthy of citizenship, at least, once they learned to "earn a living by the sweat of their brows." Senator Dawes felt Indians could achieve this Protestant virtue and introduced legislation for this end. Dawes believed that individual ownership of land, combined with a little guidance, would lead Indians quickly to civilization and preparation for citizenship. Thus, an Indian was to own a quarter section in trust for twenty-five years; then he could be given equal treatment and enjoy the liberties and responsibilities of other Americans.

There is no need to reiterate the failure of allotment, but it must be noted that the trust status of property was conceived and exists today to give Indians a special right. Moreover, the policy firmly planted the ideal that Indians should become citizens. As the aims of allotment melted away in the early 1900's (again, a war brought Indian policy to a standstill), the conception of Indians *as citizens* remained. As noted, the idea crystalized in the 1924 "Citizenship Act" which declared Indians henceforth as citizens. The Act, though, specifically did not make them strictly comparable with other Americans. Citizenship did "not in any manner impair or otherwise affect the right of an Indian to tribal or other property."

Under the Indian Reorganization Act not only were these rights recognized but the trust status of property was extended to the tribe. Allotment policy was a deliberate attempt to destroy tribal organization; the I.R.A. not only recognized the tribe but encouraged it. Tribes received charters to become incorporated for business purposes; councils were elected to represent the tribe *as a group;* and constitutions spelled out jurisdiction rights.

The I.R.A. was certainly a most humane attempt to protect former Indian rights while at the same time extending the rights of other American citizens. Although it improved economic conditions and added civil rights to Indians, the Act further complicated the nature of Indian citizenship. Given tribal jurisdiction, Indians frequently suffer injustices from which they should be protected by "due process" of law. Jurisdictional problems between tribe and state also contribute to infringement of rights. The trust status of property and treaty rights make land problems phantasmagoric and lead to major misunderstandings between Indians and whites. In the confusion, Indian rights often suffer. Finally, the special treatment accorded Indians because of cultural differences (and cultural differences were encouraged under the I.R.A.) creates special problems in the fields of education and religion. Separate analysis of each of these areas is the province of the next chapter.

Felix Cohen provides a summary of Indian special rights in a discussion of why Indians are still often considered non-citizens.[14]

> I suppose that this very widespread misimpression is a natural product of the fact that Indians are frequently not permitted to spend their own money as they please, that they frequently hold lands which are exempt from state property taxes, that on their own reservations they are generally subject to tribal customs and ordinances rather than to state criminal laws, and that they receive various services from the Federal Government . . . Now the fact is that all these legal peculiarities which we are so prone to consider marks of inferiority are either special rights which Indians have secured for themselves by contract, treaty, or statute or are incidental appendages to such special rights.

Another important aspect of these rights is made by Cohen:[15]

> The important point seems to me to be that all the peculiar legal relationships that seem to encumber the Indian are in the final analysis really obligations of the Federal Government to the Indian which only the Indian can waive. To the great majority of Indians today these special rights and privileges are of high value.

Briefly, it is possible to see some progress in the past few decades in the field of Indian civil rights. Few Indians today would think it "pretty bad" if their local Bureau superintendent could threaten them with a gun; they would not tolerate such an event. But the complexity of the situation, the misunderstanding which still exists and the inadequacy of full protection of citizenship can still be seen in testimony before Congressional committees. The following statement was made by the vice-chairman of the Lower Brule Sioux appearing before a subcommittee of the Senate Judiciary Committee in 1962.[16]

> The particular portion of my time with you here this afternoon will be spent in lieu of the fact that I have my master's degree in sociology, and I

> have been granted, given or instructed by the tribe to appear here before you. Of course, before I enter into what I am going to say, I should perhaps say that talking about a problem of any kind is good, like we have been doing this morning, and perhaps no doubt that you have been doing all this time, but, to me, it's only half good; the other half of this intention to do good starts from a proposition; the proposition then should lead to action. Unfortunately, many good intentions die in the talking stage; therefore, unless that which is discussed is proposed and acted upon, any amount of talking is a waste, for all practical purposes. My statement then will deal with an attack on the problem of what is either termed "constitutional rights or constitutional protection," and not particularly aimed at belaboring the discussion of any specific incidents which have been going on this morning. I, therefore, hope my presentation at this time isn't going to be out of context. The title of my statement, which I have written for this subcommittee to take when I get through stammering over it, is "The Need for a Legal Counselor." My statement shall be to make public a proposal which is in response to an apparently unrecognized condition which is existing for reservation Indians and nonreservation Indians. That condition is this: That they do not enjoy the same constitutional rights and constitutional protection afforded other American Citizens.

The testimony of 1929 which introduced this chapter had a comic-tragedy ring to it; the statement of this witness in 1962 is simply shocking. It points up the fact that in most Indian courts legal counsel is not only *unavailable* but in many instances is not even *allowed.* A right which is practically taken for granted by most citizens is almost unknown to Indian citizens. The next chapter analyzes some of the areas in which Indians lack the civil rights of other Americans.

chapter 4

# PROBLEMS IN THE CIVIL RIGHTS OF AMERICA'S "SPECIAL" CITIZENS

The preceding chapters were meant to give some understanding why Indians possess certain rights not due other American citizens. Because of the events which led to this unique position, Indians have found themselves often failing to secure the rights guaranteed U.S. citizens. In some cases it may be that Indians will simply have to forego former privileges if they are to secure full constitutional protections. For the most part, however, compromise and clarifying legislation can guarantee both their "special" rights and standard civil rights. Solutions will not be simple. The complexity of the problems can be seen in these most important areas: due process, jurisdictional disputes, land rights, education and religion.

I. **Due Process.** As noted in the last chapter, Indians may be tried in a court where legal counsel is not only unavailable but prohibited. This practice is only one of many which makes an Indian court unique. Three types of courts exist in Indian communities. In the United States there are fifty-three tribal courts established by constitutions or ordinances under the I.R.A.; twelve courts of Indian offenses established by the administrative authority of the Secretary of the Interior; and nineteen traditional courts among the Pueblo Indians of New Mexico. These traditional courts are governed by custom; since they are limited to the Pueblos, they will not be discussed here.

The tribal courts have been modeled after the courts of Indian offenses. The Subcommittee on Constitutional Rights found little resemblance between these courts and those of the State or Federal government.[17] The Subcommittee noted that a trial by jury was possible only if a trial judge found a substantial question of fact involved. Then, only six serve on the jury; only three of the jurors picked from the venire may be challenged. The verdict may be by majority vote. No provision is made for a grand jury. Furthermore, on most reservations there was no right to appeal. Trial judges sit together when and where they decide to hear appeals; the court is given the right to decide the manner of appeal. Since few reservations have more than one trial judge, the judge of the appeals court is usually the same individual who heard the original case. Until recently, attorneys were not allowed even in the courts of Indian offenses, but a U.S. district court has ruled this practice unconstitutional. However, rules prohibiting attorneys are still contained in most tribal constitutions or bylaws; therefore, the individual Indian's right to counsel and due process, as a *U.S. citizen*, may still be violated.

The Subcommittee concluded in its examination of Indian courts that:[18]

> It would seem, therefore, that if the Indian is to be educated in the rights and obligations with which other citizens are so familiar, he must be free to exercise these on the reservation as well as off it. Since the courts have indicated that it is unclear to what extent the Indian's constitutional rights are protected from arbitrary tribal authority, clarifying legislation may be necessary.

What this legislation may be, however, is far from clear. At first glance, such practices as lack of counsel and adequate appeal procedure seem incongruous with American citizenship. Yet, the Indians' tribal courts do have advantages. Indians are not wholly dissatisfied with them. The argument for the tribal courts was ably presented by tribal attorney before the Subcommittee on Constitutional Rights, Owen Panner. Mr. Panner was defending the court system of the Warm Springs Indians specifically, but his testimony applies generally.[19]

> The Warm Springs Tribe has its own tribally supported law and order program, and my remarks will be limited to Indians' rights in the tribal courts. We have a law and order code which was adopted in 1947 pursuant to the tribe's constitution and bylaws.

Under this code there is a chief judge and three associate judges who are appointed by the tribal council for terms of 4 years, which is in turn elected by the people every 3 years. None of these judges are attorneys and, in fact, there are no members of the tribe who have had any legal education. Nonetheless, all are represented, and tribal members are unanimous in their wish to carry on the tribal law and order program, as it now exists.

The maximum penalty permissible is 6 months in jail and a fine of $360. Without question, some defendants have disagreed with the decision of the court, but I have never known one who disagreed with the system, or with the continuation of law and order in the law and order provisions made for a jury trial.

Provision is made for a jury trial in any case on request of the defendant. If the defendant wishes assistance in the defense of the charges, he obtains a spokesman to present his or her case. Such spokesmen are not professional attorneys, but they are familiar with the Indian tongue, the court procedures, the Indian customs, and the law and order code.

No attorney prosecutes the case against the defendant. The judge simply calls witnesses for each side. After the witnesses have told their story, the defendant, or his spokesman, has the opportunity to argue his case to the jury.

Keeping in mind that the jurisdiction of the court is limited to cases which would in effect be misdemeanors, it is my firm conviction that justice prevails substantially more often than in misdemeanor trials in the State Courts.

The imposition upon the tribal courts of all the requirements of due process as we non-Indians know them, would mean the end of our tribal courts. If the defendant were represented by a professional attorney, the tribe would be required to employ a professional attorney to prosecute. All of us who have seen attorneys on opposite sides in the State courts where the justice of the peace was a layman realize that this is a hopeless situation.

If attorneys are on each side, it is imperative that there be an attorney to act as judge. On the modest budget available to the Warm Springs Tribe this becomes an impossibility, and I suspect this financial limitation would be insurmountable by the great majority of the tribes.

Mr. Panner's testimony makes it clear that the problem of protecting the Indian's right of due process is no simple matter. That is, injustice could be done if tribal courts were suddenly modeled after state courts. However, Mr. Panner's intimation that Indians are satisfied with the *status quo* is misleading. Many Indians are dissatisfied with proceedings in the tribal courts, and many are demanding the rights afforded U.S. citizens. Some change is essential, but appropriate compromises are yet to be found.

II. **Jurisdictional Problems.** One attempt to improve the judicial process on reservations is to transfer legal jurisdiction from the tribes to the states. This step would introduce such rights as trial by jury, but the major reason for transfer is believed to be improved law enforcement at the police level. Tribal police are often poorly trained, subject to many informal sanctions and generally held in low regard. Indian crime rates are notoriously high (one-third of the inmates in South Dakota state penitentiaries are Indians; Indians are only five per cent of the population). One easy answer is poor law enforcement. Obviously, the problem is far more complex; it has been well explored for one state.[20] Because of the high crime rate and other reasons, the transfer of law and order processes from the tribes to the states has been given much consideration. Congress has passed enabling legislation; but states have been slow to assume the responsibility. Partly, the hesitation is a fear of the costs involved, but the states have also met with Indian opposition.

At the American Indian Chicago Conference, Indians expressed much concern about transfer of jurisdiction. In their report they stated: "In view of the termination policy and particularly Public Law 280 [which would allow states to assume jurisdiction], many Indian people have been vitally concerned and fearful that their law and order systems will be supplanted, without their consent, by state law enforcement agencies which, perhaps, might be hostile toward them.[21]

This statement seems fairly typical. Much of the Indian fear is that they will receive unfair treatment because of prejudicial law officers. The extent of discrimination against Indians in one state has been documented.[22] What is most interesting is that in opposition to transfer of jurisdiction, Indians give secondary importance to the problem of cultural differences. They seem quite willing to change some of their legal procedures provided they are guaranteed their rights as U.S. citizens.

Emphasis upon these rights, however, could easily destroy many of the advantages which occur in the tribal courts. In a publication of the Fund for the Republic such a position seems to have developed. For instance, the report criticizes the power of the tribe in this way:[23]

> Neither Congress nor the States may infringe upon the basic civil rights of Indians, for they enjoy the same protection in respect to these governments as all other American citizens. But the Federal judiciary has determined that the guarantees of freedom of worship, speech, and the press, the right to assemble and petition the Government, and due process do not restrict tribal action. Thus, a U.S. court has held that the Navajo could enforce tribal legislation prohibiting the possession or use of peyote on the reservation, even though the ban interfered with the observance of a religion [Native American Church v. The Navajo Tribal Council, 1960]; nor can a deprivation of religious liberty be redressed under the Civil Liberties Act [Toledo v. Pueblo of Jemez, 1954]. Similarly, the amendments which forbid the United States and the States to deprive any person of life, liberty, or property without due process of law do not apply to a tribe's conduct of criminal trials [Talton v. Mayes, 1896].

No government of whatever kind should have the authority to infringe upon fundamental civil liberties; government itself must ever be subject to law. Freedom of religion, utterance, and assembly, the right to be protected in one's life, liberty, and property against arbitrary government action and to be immune from double jeopardy and bills of attainder, and the guarantee of a fair trial are not privileges; they are minimum conditions which all Americans should enjoy. For any tribe to override any of them violates the very assumptions on which our free society was established.

The complexity of the problem and the different viewpoints on solutions were examined in detail by the Task Force on Indian Affairs. Since the report is likely to be the basis of future policy, it should be examined in detail. The report notes that tribal law forces vary widely in their effectiveness, many of them being inadequate. Courts of Indian Offenses as well as tribal courts were criticized for poorly prepared judges, absence of attorneys, non-use of courts in civil actions, inadequate appellate provisions, denial of civil rights and favoritism.

However, the task force noted that the majority of Indians appearing before them believed civil and criminal jurisdiction should remain in the Federal government; no transfer to the states should occur without the *consent* of the Indians concerned; when transfer had occurred many of the involved Indians felt disappointment in the deterioration of legal protection. The report noted that some states which sought jurisdiction were unable to spend additional money for law enforcement while the Federal government, in attempting to integrate Indians into the larger society, had curtailed law and order services. Task force members criticized the effect: "The result, in the opinion of the Task Force, has often been inferior protection of life and property, denial of civil rights, and toleration of lawlessness."[24]

In conclusion, the tribal courts and courts of Indian offenses were seen as transitional and the system of divided jurisdiction as unsatisfactory. To improve the situation the Task Force made the following recommendations:

1. That Public Law 83-280 be amended to provide for the transfer of jurisdiction to the states only on the basis of negotiated agreement between the Federal government, the appropriate state governments, and the tribal governments affected. We feel this is an essential principle of the American way and a step which is necessary to remove Indian fears of unilateral termination.

2. That the Branch of Law and Order of the Bureau of Indian Affairs be directed to develop programs with the tribes and the state governments looking toward a revision of the tribal codes and the organization of tribal courts bring themselves as nearly as possible into accord with the civil and criminal codes of the states in which they are located.

3. That immediate steps be taken by the Bureau of Indian Affairs in cooperation with appropriate state governments, tribal governments,

**and Congressional committees to prepare step-by-step transfers of jurisdiction to the states in selected causes of civil and criminal action.**

4. **That the Secretary of the Interior insist that Constitutional guarantees of civil rights be observed in the Courts of Indian Offenses which are bound by his own regulations. We further think that it is incumbent upon the tribal governments which have created tribal courts under the I.R.A. to provide for protection of these rights by their own ordinances.**

The recommendations of the Task Force take into account the advantages and disadvantages of both tribal and state jurisdictions. If the recommended goals can be achieved, they will likely satisfy most Indians and others concerned with civil rights. Unfortunately, the recommendations are quite general; the particular steps and the detailed legislation are still forthcoming. Protection of former rights and constitutional rights will not be a simple matter.

III. **Indian Lands.** An equally complex problem involving Indian rights is the matter of land. On the one hand a fantastically complex technical problem has grown out of inherited trust land. Multiple heirs hold an undivided interest in much land, and compensation for use on purchase of the land is difficult. For instance, when one 116-acre tract of land was condemned on the Crow Creek Reservation for the Fort Randall Dam, ninety-nine heirs had some claim in the tract. Two received $535.67; five others received thirty-seven cents. To compute the final settlement the B.I.A. had to use a fraction whose denominator was 54,268,714,886,400. The major shareholder's interest in the 116 acres was figured at

$$\frac{4,199,364,842,400}{54,268,714,886,400}$$

On the other hand, land in trust status is a symbol of the Indian's special tie to the government. To many Indians, trust lands represent the Federal government's obligation to provide such services as education and health care. Furthermore, reservation lands symbolize something that can only be termed "Indianess." Many Indians feel strongly that their culture and identity can only be preserved as long as there is a reservation. Therefore, the reservation is more than a home; it is a vital part of the community's identity *as Indian.*

The importance of special rights in reservation real estate is illustrated by a closely connected right. Recently, Indians have argued strongly for their exclusion from state game rules. On the reservation Indians feel they are not bound by state hunting or fishing regulations. Only rarely is game of any importance in reservation economies. Recent protests have clearly been demonstrations to show the possession of special rights; the hunting or fishing in themselves were unimportant. Exclusion from state rules is, like land, symbolic of a community being Indian.

Unlike game rights, however, special ownership of land creates a paradox for Indians. Although the Supreme Court has ruled that the trust nature of property is compatible with U.S. citizenship, the special status clearly sets limits on citizens' rights. The peculiar ownership of land has meant the need for tribal courts which have not followed due process, *etc.* The Federal government's provision of other services has likewise affected civil rights. Although basic problems are created by trust provisions, ending trusteeship is no solution. Much Indian land would be lost and state governments would replace the Federal government. Both events are seen by Indians as a serious threat because of all that land symbolizes for them.

It seems likely that the problem of trusteeship will be tackled piecemeal. In the report of the Task Force land problems are closely connected with economic development, or the trust status is linked with problems of jurisdiction or self-government. It may be that a major mistake will be made if this direction is followed. Trusteeship underlies most Indian "problems" in one subtle fashion or another. For instance, it makes local self-government impossible – an issue to be examined in Chapter 6. The trust status also has set severe limits on the education services provided by the Federal government, and education, of course, is basic to a minority's acquisition of its civil rights.

IV. **Education.** The Senate Subcommittee on Constitutional Rights recognized lack of education as basic to most Indian problems. They noted in particular that inadequate education resulted in a denial or violation of rights. They illustrated this point by testimony of an Indian attorney.

> I think the judge honestly believes the Indian understands what he is saying because he spells it out for him . . . You say to an Indian with little or no education, "You are entitled to be confronted by the witness against you. You are entitled to cross-examine them." Why you might as well be speaking German to him because he doesn't know what you are talking about.[25]

Another aspect of education involves the question of integrated classrooms. Indians have not pressed for integrated schools; in fact, they appear to prefer segregation. However, it should be remembered that the "segregated" school is symbolic of the government's special tie with Indians; termination of the schools appears to Indians as simply one more step toward ending Federal obligations.

Moreover, the federal schools are often superior to rural state schools Indians would attend. Also, neighboring schools frequently are reluctant to accept Indians because of still existing prejudice. Only when the federal government's contribution – in the form of tuition for Indian pupils – more than covers the cost of education, do local schools seem quite willing to accept Indian children. In too many cases, Indian parents rightfully fear that their children will be the victims of prejudice.

Another problem involving integration is the isolation of most reservations. Indian communities are generally units unto themselves, and the schools in these communities are naturally segregated. In this regard the Task Force on Indian Affairs concluded:

> . . . The Task Force favors the location of schools as close as possible to the Indian people. While it admits the desirability of integrating Indian youngsters into the public school system, it does not believe small children should be transported long distances by bus, housed in off-reservation dormitories, or placed in public schools which do not meet the standards of those maintained by the Bureau.[26]

If this recommendation be made policy, it will still be some time before school integration is accomplished.

Perhaps the most important matter in regard to education is the lack of control and involvement on the part of Indians. The schools on reservations are a part of the Bureau hierarchy. All school personnel are subject to the bureaucracy, not to the local community being served. As a result, Indians take little part and seldom show concern over what goes on in the schools, although they place a great value on education and have much pride in their children's graduation. This problem has been analyzed in depth by Wax and Wax.[27] They show how little comprehension Indian parents have of their children's education and how lack of involvement in the system negates many of the aims of education.

The Task Force clearly recognized this problem and called for its solution.

> In connection with the establishment of school districts on Indian reservations, the Bureau must make a greater effort to involve Indian parents in school planning. The Task Force is not satisfied that simply encouraging tribes to form educational committees is sufficient. The parents of youngsters attending schools must be allowed to participate in the formulation of school programs. Wherever parent-teacher groups have not been formed, they should be established as rapidly as possible. If our goal is the ultimate transfer of educational responsibility to local school districts, then the Bureau must do everything it can now to help Indian parents learn of their rights and duties with respect to schools. The time to begin providing them such assistance is not after the transfer, but before.[28]

Again, the goals of the Task Force are laudable, but the particulars in the solution are yet to be determined. Responsibility for the school programs must be transferred, at least in part, to the community while economic support comes from the Federal government. To divorce financial responsibility from other responsibilities is always difficult.

V. **Religion.** Mission churches on reservations parallel schools in problems of responsibility. A board of missions or other national body which finances an Indian church finds it difficult to allow the local control which a non-mission church may have. Likewise, participation and involvement in the Indian church suffers just as schools suffer. In this regard, missions resemble the Bureau of Indian Affairs.[29] This problem, of course, is not one of civil rights, but Indians could be learning more responsibility in their churches as preparation for assuming control over other areas of their life. Furthermore, if missions found some way of delegating major responsibility to local churches while still providing necessary monetary support, a model for the Federal government, faced with a similar problem, might be provided.

However, the major civil rights problem in regard to religion is the use of peyote by the Native American Church. In the 19th Century many "pagan" practices were prohibited arbitrarily by the Bureau; since the 1930's, however, there has been little interference with Indian faiths except for the Native American Church. Opposition to the Church is overtly based on the fact that peyote, which produces unusual biological effects, is used as a sacrament. One may wonder, however, if there may not be some covert opposition because of the strength and popularity of the Church among Indians.

Whatever the basis of the opposition, an important question of civil liberty is involved. Many states do or had outlawed use or possession of peyote. (Federal laws do not label peyote as a narcotic; it can be sent through the U.S. mails.) Even if it were a narcotic, the question remains: Can a religious practice be prohibited by the state? The California State Supreme Court has held that religious *practices*, but not *beliefs*, can be abridged under the First Amendment. This matter has yet to be decided by the Supreme Court.

However, at the state level the trend has been for the courts to interpret the prohibiting of peyote within the church as unconstitutional. Thus, the California court's most recent ruling is that the California legislature did not have the right to ban the use of peyote as a sacrament. The court pointed out that the state had no right to make Indians conform to mass society. In Arizona a similar judgement was rendered by the Superior Court of Coconino County. In the decision it was pointed out that, ". . . the practical effect of the statute outlawing [peyote's] use is to prevent worship by members of the Native American Church . . . The manner in which peyote is used by the Indian worshipper is not inconsistent with the public health, morals, or welfare."[30]

Although it appears likely that the threat to religious freedom from state governments is on the wane, no relief is seen from tribal ordinances which may violate rights of citizens. This danger was well expressed by the Subcommittee on Constitutional Rights.

> Of no less importance than the alleged denial of religious freedom resulting from the Navajo tribal ordinance is the question of a tribe's authority to restrict the liberties guaranteed citizens under the Federal Constitution. Thus, the Secretary of the Interior in approving various tribal ordinances and resolutions, may be sanctioning denials of individual rights guaranteed Indians under the U.S. Constitution.
>
> The extent to which a tribe may abrogate a federally protected constitutional right and the limits upon the Federal government's authority to intervene in tribal affairs have been tested recently in two suits brought in the Federal courts concerning the prohibition of the Navajo tribal ordinance against the use of peyote. The question is of major consequence because of its relationship to the Constitution, as construed by the Supreme Court which – "acknowledges the paramount authority of the United States with regard to Indian tribes but recognizes the existence of Indian tribes as *quasi* sovereign possessing all the inherent rights of sovereignty excepting where restrictions have been placed thereon by the United States itself. (Iron Crow vs. Ogala Sioux Tribe of Pine Ridge Reservation, 231 F. Sd. 89, 92, 1956.)
>
> In reaching this decision, the courts hold that they possess no jurisdiction over the ordinances of the Navajo Tribal Council. These decisions do not, however, resolve the fundamental and increasingly important question of how an individual Indian, as a citizen, can protect himself against a tribal government whose actions allegedly violate the Federal Constitution. These decisions indicate that the question of tribal regulations of constitutional rights can only be solved through the enactment of legislation.

Thus, problems of even religious freedom are closely linked with Executive policy and Supreme Court decisions which defined the status of Indian tribes. The historical background of Indian and Federal government relations is vital for understanding all present civil rights conflicts. However, much more is involved than the chronology of events. The nature of the modern Indian community, the structure of Bureau-Indian relations and culture differences are also important factors which must be examined in order to evaluate what might be done to protect Indian civil rights. In the following chapters these factors and their relationship with civil rights are examined.

chapter 5

# CIVIL RIGHTS IN THE SMALL COMMUNITY

Although many of our civil rights and liberties were defined by men who could not be described as urban, conditions were such that rights were defined for life in an impersonal world. Ideas such as "Justice is Blind," "All Men are Equal," and so on, were the basis for the Bill of Rights. The civil rights that sprang from these sources relied heavily upon formal forces of control such as the courts and police. As our nation became more and more urban and impersonal, reliance on these forces was greater, and the civil rights which we prize now become more and more adapted to impersonality.

To lift these rights from their urban or national context and place them wholesale in the small community will not only wreck traditional forms of social control but may also bring injustice. Tribal peoples, in particular, are likely to suffer because of manipulation of the larger society's rule on the part of a few individuals. Even in the small, personal Anglo community "due process" may not be as "just" and certainly not as effective as sanctions such as gossip, ridicule or reminders of kinship obligations.

In regard to Indian communities some American civil rights may not only be lacking but even inapplicable. For instance, on the Lower Brule reservation the tribal policeman believed that he had authority over Lower Brule members alone. If an Anglo were to commit an offense on the reservation, the county sheriff could be summoned, but if an Indian from another reservation violated the law, there was no one to assume jurisdiction. The tribal policeman said he resolved the problem by putting such an offender in his car, claiming he was taking him to the county jail. When he had driven far enough from the reservation boundary that the "arrested" Indian could not return, the policeman released him with a threat not to return.[31] This procedure is a far cry from due process, yet it was the only alternative available to the policeman. Actually, the policeman did have proper jurisdiction in such a case under a ruling of the Bureau. However, being unaware of the ruling, the officer had no other recourse. Moreover, there is some question as to whether the Bureau had proper authority to make such a ruling. The Bureau has provided regulations governing the behavior of Indians on reservations other than their own, but the authority for this jurisdiction is unclear.

More important than formal sources of power is the question of what is justice in the highly personal world of the small community. Numerous cases have pointed up the great injustices people have suffered through gossip and scandal. Notably, school teachers have been persecuted in small towns without redress to the law. On the other hand, the little community may often enforce justice by informal sanctions more effectively than could the law. At any rate, the use of non-legal means to accomplish what the community thinks is "right", is certainly not confined to Indian reservations.

James West describes how a small, Midwest town once dealt with its problems.[32]

> Few people now condemn the laws dealing with murder, but a generation ago many upheld "feud law". A retired preacher recounted tales of a dozen murders that had occurred within his memory. He and many other people knew the motives and details of each murder, but when officers came into the community to investigate, practically everybody questioned withheld all important information. Part of this unwillingness to cooperate came from fear of reprisals by kinsmen of the guilty, but part of it came from the feeling that men should be allowed to settle disputes in their own way. Some cases finally reached trial, but few men were convicted, and no convicted man spent over four years in the penitentiary. If a murder occurred today, people would still try to avoid telling what they knew about it.

The reluctance to become involved in the courtroom is common to most Americans, but what is of importance here is the feeling that formal, legal sanctions are inappropriate. Members of the small community fail to see the law as significant in most aspects of their life. West points out that, "The role of actual legal organization among all other mechanisms which force

Plainvillers to conform to their society's established patterns of behavior is really very slight. More important mechanism, both preventive and punitive, for social control are gossip, ridicule, and, in the widest sense of the term, folklore."

The lack of formal, legal means of control is documented also for a small Anglo community of New Mexico.[33] Vogt tells that Homestead (pseudonym for the town) had a deputy sheriff and Justice of the Peace in the late 1930's, but both were ineffective and participated in feuds. He reports this case:

> One time the Justice of the Peace got drunk and chased the preacher around the Community Church with a knife. I and two others got together and went down to see him after this happened and told him he'd have to pay a fine. The deputy refused to arrest him and take him to court, so I went down to get him myself and took him over to Tapala (the Spanish-American village) but they didn't have any Justice of Peace over there then. So then we took him down to the Justice of Peace at Ventana. A number of cars of people from Homestead went along. A bunch of the women piled up enough charges agin' our Justice to hang him. When they rattled off all these charges, the Justice at Ventana said they would be too much for him to handle, and they'd have to take him to the county seat. But no one wanted to take him all the way to Los Lunas, so the women withdrew most of their charges and jest charged him with disturbin' the peace. So the Justice fined him $5 and everybody went home. Then, after they left, the Justice filled up my pickup with gas and gave our Justice the $5 back!

When the deputy and Justice moved from Homestead their positions went unfilled for several years. Once a deputy was appointed, he made no arrests. On one occasion, when he attempted to stop a fight, the participants all turned on him. Another time the deputy appeared when a Homesteader "went crazy". He was told to go home and "mind his own business". The insane man was cared for by a group of informal leaders who took the man to the state hospital.

Informal punitive action in Homestead consists, in mild cases, of perennial gossip. This gossip not only punishes offenders but stresses important values and reinforces the social system. Where gossip is ineffective, resort may be made to fist fighting. Vogt stresses that this violence is not uncontrolled force but follows clear-cut rules for settlement of disputes. Finally, where violations of the values are serious, informal leaders will gather the disputants for a long talk and if no solution is found, resort is finally made to the Justice of the Peace in a nearby community. State police or the county sheriff are never called.

This situation cannot be seen as totally unjust simply because an individual is denied his rights under the due process clause of the constitution. Homestead is certainly not a "lawless" or un-American community. Vogt points out that, "The rejection of the law represented by outside authorities does not mean that the Homesteader is 'lawless'; indeed, he feels that he is a moral and law-abiding person. Rather, it means that the Homesteader's definition of what constitutes 'crime' varies at many points with the county and state legal definitions. Further, it indicates that the controls for deviant and 'lawless' behavior are present within the community."[34]

If civil rights are so often violated in Anglo communities where individuals are generally aware of their "rights", it should be no surprise that civil rights problems are even more complex in the modern Indian community. Not only is there frequent ignorance of rights, but there are frequent contradictions of what is considered "right". Former Indian values may be incompatible with Anglo values. Not only do different groups of Indians come into conflict because one faction holds to the former while others adapt the new, but also an individual may accept Anglo values in one social context while adhering to aboriginal values in another context.

The interpretation of Anglo and Indian values, the confusion over legal process and problems of proper jurisdiction may all be seen in the following case. It also illustrates the irony of people in a highly personal world accepting processes which are best adapted for an impersonal, urban world.

In 1960, at Lower Brule the Bureau of Indian Affairs had appointed a judge who was convinced that the state of South Dakota was going to assume jurisdiction over the reservation. He believed it his duty to introduce some of the procedures he thought were followed in state courts. He was most critical of the former judge who simply heard both sides of a case, was already well familiar with the dispute, and whose judgements were often based on old Indian values. The new judge explained how he had handled one of his first cases.

> You know that X family. They had neglected their children for years. I finally told the policeman he better bring them in. I set their bail at $10. They paid it and went home. When it came time for the trial, they never showed up. So I took their bail money and sent the policeman over after them. (The home of X is within sight from where court is held.) They thought that bail money was their fine, but they'll just have to learn. Then I asked them if they had counsel. They said, "No, we don't like any of those people on the (tribal) council." I tried to explain about a lawyer. Since they didn't have one, I told them I would act as their counsel. Of course, we don't have a prosecuting attorney either so I had to prosecute the case. It was our first jury trial. I only had six people instead of twelve. It was hard to find people who weren't related to the X's and who would be fair. My mother was on the jury. I suppose that might not be right since I was the judge, but she's fair and she's known the X's all their life.[35]

This judge was a fairly well educated man for his community. He had served overseas in the Second World War, had made many friends among whites and had lived off the reservation on occasion. Still, most of his knowledge of courtroom procedure probably is derived from TV shows, such as "Perry Mason." Even if he had some special training as a judge, the problems of a small, rural kinship-knit community would remain. No lawyers are readily available; the "facts" of a case are quickly spread by rumor and issues largely "solved" by gossip. A judge, and certainly jury members, are going to be related to the defendant and plaintiff in some way; the Lower Brule have an expression, "We are all relatives here." To ask for a change of venue is impossible. It is only the tribe which has jurisdiction.

It is indeed difficult to see how civil rights such as due process are going to be introduced into many Indian communities. Social control in the small community simply makes impractical some constitutional guarantees. The problem is compounded in the Indian tribe where the rights are misunderstood, where cultural values of right and wrong may differ sharply and where confusion over federal, state and tribal authority is rampant.

Furthermore, the reluctance of Indians to accept the justice and legal process of the surrounding society is heightened by their treatment in the outside world. Oliver LaFarge has noted a number of shocking cases of injustice done Indians in state courts.[36] Only a few of his instances are necessary to point up the Indians' fear of treatment in courts where civil rights are supposedly guaranteed.

> North Dakota takes its name from one of the Great Plains Indian tribes. There not long ago . . . an Indian named William Demerce was drinking with two non-Indians, Nicholas Ramos and Alcario Garcia. They got into a fight in the course of which Demerce was stabbed to death. His companions got ***ninety days apiece for disorderly conduct.***
>
> In one South Dakota town, an Indian failed to stop one night when a policeman challenged him. The policeman shot him; then, as he lay in the gutter, wounded, ran up and finished him off with two more shots. So far as we can learn, no action was taken against the officer. The Indian Service investigated but was powerless to get anything done.
>
> Incidents occur, such as the recent killing of a Sioux named Broken Rope by a local chief of police, in which a clear legal case cannot be made, but one who reads the account is forced to conclude that, had the subjects been white men, they would not have been so used.
>
> More clear-cut is an incident involving a Mr. Fred Stotts. Mr. Stotts was in his home when he seized a baseball bat, ran out and across the street, and bashed a Sioux named George Left Hand Bull over the head so hard he crushed his skull. We may assume that Mr. Stotts disliked Mr. Left Hand Bull, but the available record does not tell why. Mr. Stotts had the Sioux tossed in the clink where, without medical attention, he died the next day. The white man was arrested and charged with manslaughter for which, in due course, having pleaded guilty, he received a ***two-year suspended sentence.***

The only thing that can be said for insuring civil rights of Indians in courts is that the matter is far off, and no simple solution is possible. Legal procedure in any small community is going to give way, at least in part, to sanctions such as gossip, ridicule, ostracism and back-biting. For some time, even witchcraft will serve in some Indian communities. Certainly, the transfer of jurisdiction from the tribe to the state will not immediately solve the problem and, if hastily done, will likely bring more injustice. Not only are Indians largely unaware of their rights in state courts, but a fear of the white man's world would make them helpless in such a situation. Moreover, Indians would undoubtedly suffer from still existing, strong prejudices among local law enforcement officers, jury members and even court officials. The situation requires not only thoughtful and well-planned legislation but also careful study and research. Development of the field will be linked with whatever happens to self-government in Indian communities, which is the subject of the next chapter.

chapter 6

# RIGHTS TO SELF-GOVERNMENT IN INDIAN COMMUNITIES

Although self-government usually is not a part of present civil rights discussions, it must be considered in the case of Indian reservations. Other minorities, especially the Negro, are refused the right to vote; Indians experience little difficulty, but the officials they elect have little or no power. (Full participation in state and national elections was not always possible for Indians even after they were made citizens, but all states now grant them the franchise. There have been few complaints of discrimination at the polls.)

The major handicap is that decisions in an Indian community are made by outsiders. The representatives or tribal council members act almost solely as consulting or advisory bodies. Real control remains in the Bureau of Indian Affairs. About the only way Indians can bring pressure to bear on Bureau representatives is through their Congressmen. Although some Indians have become unusually adroit at this method, it is a most cumbersome and lengthy process. Needless to say, it is also far from democratic.

The events leading to this lack of self-government have been briefly described in the preceding chapters. As noted, much jurisdiction remains in Indian hands and theoretically, under tribal constitutions, governing bodies should have much control over community actions. Actually, however, the Bureau of Indian Affairs makes most decisions for Indian communities because of the trust status of Indian property. The Bureau acts much as an executor would over property inherited by a minor; it is responsible for the use of trust land or income derived from that land. Furthermore, because this land is tax exempt, the federal government must provide services usually assumed by the county and state. States are reluctant to assume responsibility for trust lands because reservations are generally overpopulated and underdeveloped. Taxes on such land would be insufficient to furnish the services Indians now receive. As a result, the Bureau of Indian Affairs retains its responsibilities and tribal councils, or other governing bodies of Indians, never can be fully self-governing. The federal government is responsible ultimately for almost all expenditures and decisions that Indian governing bodies make; therefore, it must retain ultimate control. The short phrase "subject to the approval of the Secretary of the Interior" appears innocuous enough in tribal constitutions, but it appears in such places that it renders true self-government impossible.

A case study of one Indian community's politics will illustrate the weakness of self-government under Indian Reorganization Act provisions. This case is provided by Robert Thomas, an anthropologist who studied the Pine Ridge Reservation at length. His analysis of Sioux government was presented to the 1964 American Anthropological Association as a paper entitled "Powerless Politics." Mr. Thomas, who also served as a consultant for this report, has described the political structure of an Indian community so well that his results are worth quoting at length.

"Nearly all former (Pine Ridge Sioux) institutions on the local level have disappeared. The small Sioux community is hardly even a community. It is a kin group without the aboriginal institutions which once related them to their environment, and no substitute institutions have developed in their place. New institutions have been preempted by outsiders. The old Chief's Council is non-functional. The warriors' societies have long since disappeared and the local police force is seen as a foreign and illegitimate coercive force. Thus, few (practically no) means of social control are left to local Sioux community. There are no local school boards – the schools are run by the federal government. Their churches are controlled by an outside religious hierarchy. Economic institutions are virtually non-existent. The only really functional institutions are the old native religious groups which have carried over from aboriginal times. It is in this context that Sioux opinion leaders are developed.

"A major institution, which has been in recent years introduced into the community by the federal authorities, is the tribal government. From the viewpoint of the country Sioux, this new institution is "The Tribe." In many ways they look at it in the same way that many urban working class people look at the police force and city government. They see it as a foreign coercive feature in their daily lives. To the older Sioux, the tribal government gets in the way of their personal approach to the powerful and benevolent federal government. The country Sioux certainly do not see the tribal council as representing them nor as making decisions for them. Tribal councilmen are elected to 'get something' from the Bureau of Indian Affairs. The country Sioux are poor people, and being in tribal government pays well so there are always volunteers for these offices. The criterion for selection of tribal councilmen by those few Sioux who do vote in an election is not that the tribal councilman can represent them or their opinion, but because they feel that a particular person knows how to handle whites and can 'get something' for the Sioux. A tribal councilman thus may be tremendously competent or incompetent, socially responsible or irresponsible. Invariably, they are very marginal to the community and sometimes even personally disliked. No sooner does the new tribal administration go into office than charges of dishonesty and 'half-breeds' are hurled at them by the country Sioux, and in the next election they usually 'turn the rascals out'.

"But let us take a look at this institution from an outside viewpoint. In form, this is an urban American institution. Such procedures as majority rule, representative government, and voting are evidence of this. Many of these forms and procedures are very foreign to Sioux life. Even the voting districts which have been laid off do not correspond to any meaningful social units. This, of course, is not an overwhelming handicap since many tribal peoples all over the world today are learning to operate and function in institutions which are urban in form. The tribal government is, however, called upon to make more decisions in the economic sphere than is usual in urban America.

"But the main difference between Sioux tribal government and government in other American communities is that the Sioux tribal government is, in effect, without power. Most of the day to day decisions about Sioux life, about roads, schools, relief, are made by Bureau personnel. And information about such decisions are in Bureau files. Further, what decision the tribal council makes is subject to approval by the Secretary of Interior.

"Local whites are very well aware of who holds the power and the purse strings on the Pine Ridge Indian reservation. And when local whites come to

Pine Ridge on business they first go to see the local superintendent. A white banker or a mayor of a small town literally has no way to relate to the tribal council and usually no real reason to enter into a relationship. Ranchers and cowboys no longer set the tone for white society in this area. It is now the judgements of the small town middle class that the Sioux must face. It is hard for these people to see the Sioux as anything but incompetent. They see Sioux affairs being run for them by a federal bureaucracy; and they perceive the Sioux leaders as perpetually haranguing and 'wheedling' the government for special privilege.

"In a larger sense, the tribal government is an arm of the Bureau of Indian Affairs. The local police chief, when I was on Pine Ridge reservation, was a member of another tribe and a federal employee, not responsible either to the tribal government nor to his constituency. One only has to look at the layout of the town of Pine Ridge to see how much the tribal government is an adjunct of the local Bureau. The town of Pine Ridge is divided into two sections. The east side of town in 1957 was an area of tumble-down shacks in which the Sioux lived. The west side of town was the Bureau 'compound'. It was in this area along with other Bureau facilities that the tribal buildings were located.

"Let us now look at the dynamics of this institution of tribal government. As I mentioned above, from the point of view of the country Sioux, the tribal council is there not to make decisions for the Sioux, rather to get something from powerful whites. But in urban America, we have a tendency to name something; to accept a definition which goes along with the very word itself; and to act on that premise. To the local Bureau employees, the tribal government is a decision-making body, and they approach it with suggestions about programs which would be beneficial to the Sioux. The tribal councilman may indeed share with the representatives of the federal government the assumption that he is a decision maker; or he may very well know that this is not the way his constituents perceive him. Even if it is the latter, he will listen very intently to the 'suggestions' of the people who hold the power and the purse strings because he must establish his credit with them as a responsible leader in order to 'get something for the Sioux'. In any case, these suggestions are listened to very closely because everyone knows very well that the final decision of a tribal council's action is approved or disapproved by the Secretary of Interior. Most of the programs suggested to the tribal council are unfamiliar to them and are usually couched in terms which, from the viewpoint of an anthropologist, seem very well fitted for a middle class American community but at wide variance with the Sioux. Enough has been said about these kinds of programs in other parts of the world, and the lack of fit they have to another culture. These programs naturally fail to reach their desired ends and this adds to the Sioux feelings of incompetence and impotence.

"Now let us take a look at the reaction from the other end – the country Sioux. Very few governmental actions are initiated in the country Sioux community. One could say that so far as decision-making is concerned, except in the religious sphere, the Sioux community lies inert. When a decision of the tribal council such as setting up a tribal program for cattle raising begins to be heard of in the local community, the Sioux react. Since the program is unfamiliar and basically one which is fitted for a white community, the Sioux see it as un-Sioux, as dishonest; and one hears a cry raised by a majority of the people against the 'half-breeds' on the tribal council who are frittering away Sioux money and lining their own pockets. The marginal people in the community who share many things with whites, of course, see the program as beneficial and respond to it. Also, they are the ones who are in the position to most benefit from a basically American white program which is unfamiliar to the majority of the Sioux. This is the basis for factionalism among the Pine Ridge Sioux – how one responds, as a Sioux, to action initiated from outside the community."

Mr. Thomas notes that the picture he draws is bleak. He believes that the situation may improve somewhat with education and experience. A few master politicians are appearing and, as Sioux become experienced in the general society, the situation may ease.

Evidence for a such a trend has been provided by Basehart and Sasaki. They found that in recent years the Jicarilla Apache Tribal Council has taken the course indicated by Thomas. "In the past few years tribal autonomy has been fostered."[37]

However, a paradox is clearly pointed up which no amount of education or experience can solve:

> One of the most significant features of agency activities has been the education of the Jicarilla into Western ways of life through innovations of the type discussed in an earlier section. In carrying out this tutorial role, the agency has furthered the development of tribal authority and responsibility. As a result, at the present time, areas of overlapping authority and responsibility exist which lead to misunderstanding and tension between officers of the two units. The agency can resolve conflicts by the exercise of power, but action of this kind tends to undermine tribal political independence and thus the agency's own aims. Further, since the agency itself is not the sole locus of power, tribal officers may be tempted to bypass the chain of command in an effort to maintain independence of action. One might say that in this learning process, the pupil has outpaced the teacher, and that is precisely what is desired. Such statements may rationalize but do not minimize the strains that develop in situations of this kind.

> The problems presented by an imbalance in power, authority, and responsibility can be examined from another point of view through consideration of the role of the agency superintendent. As the tribe begins to engage more actively in the political process and achieves sophistication in the exercise of authority and responsibility, the *effective* authority of the superintendent is apt to decrease. At the same time, his responsibility does not diminish. The bonded superintendent is not merely regarded by his superiors as responsible; he is *legally* responsible for the performance of his trust obligations and is subject to legal suit as the accountable agent. Of course, the superintendent retains ultimate power; action initiated by the tribe in a number of areas can become effective only after his approval. Nonetheless, the degree of direct control by the superintendent declines, while his responsibility remains constant. If these two trends were to continue over time, a superintendent would find himself in the wholly untenable position of lacking any effective authority or power while continuing to have responsibility.[38]

If this paradox is to be solved and if Indians are to be made self-governing, new legislation must be passed by Congress, and details will be in the hands of lawmakers. However, it is essential that the legislation provide funds without ultimate responsibility (and therefore authority) over them. Such a step should not be construed as merely a handout to Indians. Budgeting, accounting, and other planning would have to be provided for, but Indian political units, not the Bureau of Indian Affairs would be the responsible bodies.

Many Anglo Americans appear reluctant to entrust Indians with monetary responsibility. Implicit in their view is an argument that anyone who is not financially independent is irresponsible. However, it should be remembered that Indians either chose or were forced onto land which cannot support them. Today's reservations are notably poor agricultural lands with little chance for any industrial development. More than fifty per cent of the working force on most Dakota reservations is unemployed; average Indian family income is less than $2,000. There appears little chance for major change in this situation, although the "war on poverty" does hold some promise.

The important point to remember is that historical circumstance is a major factor in the poverty of Indians. It does not follow that Indians are irresponsible simply because they are poor. Yet they are denied full self-government largely because of their poverty. It is almost as if we retracted citizenship rights of West Virginia coal miners simply because they are no longer self-supporting. Further details and full analysis of the federal relationship with Indians have been provided by Tax.[39] This brief analysis is simply to emphasize that voting privileges for Indians are not enough. The representatives they elect must have the power to make decisions comparable in importance to those made in other American communities.

chapter 7

# SELF-DETERMINATION IN INDIAN COMMUNITIES

The lack of true self-government in Indian communities means, of course, a lack of self-determination. If self-government is eventually achieved, some major problems of self-determination will remain. Problems of primary importance concern education and religion. Both of these areas have long been central in civil rights issues; however, among Indians the problems differ in detail.

Much has been written about the education of American Indians. Under John Collier several tribes were studied intensively, and extensive reports are available on the results.[40] Concise surveys of a number of general problems have been provided by Thompson[41] and Havinghurst.[42] These reports have been most useful for teachers of Indians and school administrators with the Bureau of Indian Affairs.

However, most of these studies have not touched on some aspects of education which relate to civil rights. One immediate principle which is raised in regard to Indian schools is integration. Primarily because the ill effects of segregation upon Negro children have received much attention, questions have been asked about the desirability of maintaining separate school systems for Indians. It should be noted emphatically that, in contrast with Negro education, the evidence does not indicate that Indian children suffer in the same way from having their own schools. Certainly, Indians have not demanded integrated classrooms as have Negroes. Satisfaction with the present system derives from several sources. Before examining these, however, it is necessary to describe the present educational system.

The first schools among Indians were established by missionaries. In the early 19th Century the federal government appropriated money for their support. Toward the end of the century the issue of church and state separation brought an end to the government participation. The first federal school for Indians was established in 1860. From that date federal schools grew rapidly in number, although never fast enough.

Opponents of federal involvement believed Indians incapable of acquiring an education, but sufficient friends of Indians saw that Congress appropriated money each year for the schools. This first education was by boarding school. The method deliberately attempted to remove children as far as possible from the influence of parents and Indian culture. Schools were operated much like a military academy, and discipline was strict. Older Indians frequently recall how severely they were whipped if they ever lapsed into their Indian language.

In the late 1920's opposition to the boarding schools developed largely because of the Meriam report.[43] Not only had the failure of the old system become apparent, but also advances in the social sciences pointed up the importance of family security in the development of youth. A day school program was begun which was to receive further impetus under the Indian Reorganization Act.

Although education on the reservation soon became the general pattern, the desirability of including Indians in the public schools was also being recognized. (Some Indians attended public schools much earlier, but these were exceptional cases.) In 1934, the Johnson-O'Malley Act provided authority for the government to assist public schools on the basis of financial hardship because of the tax-free nature of Indian land. Public Laws 815 and 874 have supplemented the Johnson-O'Malley Act increasing the ease of state responsibility for Indian education. This legislation led to the elimination of almost all federal Indian schools in Florida, Oregon, California, Michigan, Washington, Minnesota, Idaho, Nebraska and Wyoming. According to Thompson, ". . . any resistance on the part of state authorities and educational agencies toward acceptance of responsibility for the education of Indian children stems primarily from financial reasons and not from racial discrimination. The isolated individual resistance to Indians in the public schools is the exception, not the general attitude."[44]

Although Thompson may be correct in her assessment of the white attitude toward Indians, she has ignored the crucial factor of how Indians feel about state control over education. First, the schools have long been symbols of the federal government's obligations to Indians. Indian lands were often given up for the promise of schools; to eliminate these schools is often seen as revoking treaty rights and a step toward ending all treaty privileges. Thus, the transfer of education to the states is often interpreted by Indians as a threat to their status *as Indians.* Second, in many areas the federal schools are much better financed than state schools. Federal employees are in Civil Service positions commanding higher salaries than rural state teachers; the federal schools are generally much better constructed. In a number of areas, if Indian children were put into state schools, they would go from modern classrooms with well-paid teachers to one-room schools. The Task Force on Indian Affairs recognized this problem and recommended no transfer under such conditions. Finally, the Indian attitude toward integrated schools is far different from the Negro. Partly, Indians are not faced with far inferior schools for their children, but it must also be remembered that reservation people have chosen to keep a distinct and separate way of life. Their own school in their own community is seen as one way of preserving an Indian way of life. The schools are symbolic, then, not only of special government recognition but also of a separate community life which holds a strong value. As Indians develop a greater pride and sense of being *Indian,* their separate schools become even more valuable. To call these schools "segregated" is misleading. There is a strong positive value within the community to preserve the Indian school, and if Indians are to be allowed self-determination, then their attitudes toward the schools must be considered.

However, to allow full self-determination requires much more than preservation of the present system. If Indians are to determine what education is to mean to them, then they must be given far more control and responsibility over their school systems. Today, an Indian school is directed solely by the Bureau of Indian Affairs. Even bus drivers, cook's helpers and janitors are federal employees responsible directly to the Bureau. The local Indian community has no control over school personnel, curriculum or other planning. Although Indians take much pride in the education of their children and see the schools as "theirs" by treaty rights, they think of the schools only as an outside institution operated *for* them, not *by* them. As a result, Indians show little interest in what goes on in the classroom; their comprehension of what education *is,* is minimal. Their major interest is solely in the end product – graduation, which means a chance for the employment of their children.

Under present regulations a local Board of Education would be in the same position *vis a vis* the superintendent as the tribal council described in the last chapter. As authority was gradually transferred to a representative Indian body, responsibility of the agency superintendent should also decline. However, even nominal Boards of Education do not exist today on Indian reservations. What learning and assumption of authority is possible in tribal councils is non-existent for education. On some reservations Parent-Teacher Associations have been formed, but even in the white community this organization allows only indirect control.

If Indian education is to be made a vital part of community life and if Indian parents are to comprehend and take interest in their schools, then they must be given some authority and responsibility over education. The major problem is not a question of integrated *vs.* segregated classrooms. The Indian is denied an "equal education" because community members are powerless in determining any matters in their schools. They are not taxed at the polls or given discriminatory registration tests, but they are denied the opportunity to vote on the people or policies which determine the education of their children.

This problem has been examined at length by Wax and Wax.[45] This brief analysis can only show the uniqueness of some problems in Indian civil rights. Questions such as the "segregated" classroom cannot be resolved for Indians in the same way as they may, hopefully, be resolved for other minorities.

Another unique civil rights problem is found in religion. Although the issue is judged on state-church grounds, the basic question is how far Indians may go in determining for themselves their own religion. The major issue has been over the use of peyote, a species of cactus. It is claimed that peyote is a drug and therefore subject to state control. However, it may be questioned whether concern is strictly on health grounds. It may be that the religion which uses peyote is so different from other American religions that it will not be tolerated.

Certainly, the evidence for peyote being a drug is insubstantial. Several attempts early in the century failed in obtaining Congressional action banning the use of peyote. However, a number of states did outlaw its use. Most medical discussions of peyote have centered on mescaline, an ingredient of the plant. Mescaline causes sweating, increased reflexes, nausea and tremors. Delusions and hallucinations, especially bright color patterns, or a feeling of increased sensory perception are commonly reported. These latter symptoms are most often described by participants in the religious ceremony. It must be noted that most experiments have been confined to mescaline alone. Other properties of peyote could conceivably alter or balance the effects of mescaline.

J.S. Slotkin, an anthropologist who spent much of his life studying the Native American Church which uses peyote, concluded that:

> There is no valid scientific evidence that peyote is harmful, either mentally or physically, as there is for the injurious effects of alcohol, coffee, or tobacco, commonly used by whites. Consequently, the fact that opponents of peyote are anxious to prohibit its use, but not the popular white drugs, shows that their prejudice is entirely ethnocentric.[46]

Slotkin has been joined by other prominent anthropologists in the view that peyote cannot be considered a narcotic.

> . . . according to Webster's Dictionary a narcotic is a drug that allays sensibility, relieves pain, and produces profound sleep; an intoxicant stupefies. According to March's Manual, the symptoms of drug addiction are increased tolerance and dependence. On the basis of our experience, we would say that peyote seems to have none of these effects. It does not excite, stupefy, or produce muscular incoordination; there is no hangover; and the habitual user does not develop any increased tolerance or dependence . . .[47]

It may be some time before the legal status of peyote is clearly established. In the meantime, another strong argument against its use is raised by those who claim peyote is substituted for medicine. Slotkin meets this argument by pointing out that most Indians who are introduced to peyote for medical purposes are coming to it after all else has failed. Of course, on civil rights grounds, the argument is futile. Peyote should no more be prohibited than the faith healing in certain Christian sects or in the Christian Science Church.

In summary, religious freedom of Indians must be guaranteed the same as any other American religion. If peyote is ever proved to be a harmful narcotic, then legislation against its use may not violate the First Amendment. However, any limitations on the use of the plant must be carefully watched. For a long time it was federal policy to ban all Indian rites. Although the policy was officially reversed under the Indian Reorganization Act, local Bureau officials and neighboring whites may still exert pressure to substitute their brand of Christianity for the religious practices of Indians, particularly the Native American Church.

It should now be obvious that Indian civil rights in education and religion resemble other of their rights – they require special attention because they are in many ways unique. Today, Indians are almost totally denied any determination in their education. If they are given equal opportunity in this area, it may be that their goals and purposes will differ from the larger society in order that they may preserve some of their different values. Americans have traditionally tolerated such cultural differences, but only to a degree. In the past, the majority has placed limits on how far Indians can differ. Hopefully, the tolerance can grow, and certainly it should be such that, at least, the civil rights due all citizens are never violated.

chapter 8

# CONCLUSIONS AND RECOMMENDATIONS

A major theme of this report is that civil rights problems of American Indians are particularly complex because Indians can claim special rights. Their unique rights derive from historical circumstance. The fact that they were an indigenous people, treated as separate nations and eventually became a minority with special ties to the federal government makes them unlike any other group in the United States. Special legislation will be required to insure their civil rights as citizens. Of course, more than legislation will be needed. Social change both on the part of the minority and majority must also occur to protect Indians from now existing prejudice and discrimination.

Unfortunately, many people see the necessary social change as Indian assimilation into the larger societies. The experience of other minorities tends to justify this ideal of America as a "melting pot"; but it seems unlikely that assimilation will be the course for Indians. D'Arcy McNickle, a prominent Indian, has noted the persistence of Indian communities.

> In order to understand why Indian communities remain isolated from the main stream, we must remember that as white settlement spread to the interior, the Indian societies were like people caught in a flooding valley, moving to higher ground as the invading waters encroached upon them, until in time they were completely surrounded. Segregation was an act of self-preservation, the motivation being to keep what they had. This motivation persists. We may consider it unreasonable and self-limiting, but it is questionable whether human action is ever entirely rational and

> logical. Nor is it likely that human conduct can be changed merely by pointing out its irrationalities.[48]

McNickle's view has been given full support by most anthropologists. At a special conference on the future of Indians a number of anthropologists arrived at the conclusion:

> Most Indian groups of the United States, after more than one hundred years of Euro-American contact and in spite of strong external pressures, both direct and fortuitous, have not yet become assimilated in the sense of a loss of community identity and the full acceptance of American habits of thought and conduct. No one can expect such group assimilation within any short, predictable time period, say one to four generations. The urge to retain tribal identity is strong and operated powerfully for many Indian groups. It finds support in some of the attitudes and behavior of the general American public, and has been encouraged by Federal policy for the past twenty years. Group feeling and group integrity among the American Indians are as likely to gain strength in the decades ahead as they are to lose it.
>
> . . . The conference agreed that despite external pressures, and internal change, most of the present identifiable Indian groups residing on reservations (areas long known to them as homelands) will continue indefinitely as distinct social units, preserving their basic values, personality, and Indian way of life, while making continual adjustments, often superficial in nature, to the economic and political demands of the larger society . . .[49]

The issue of special rights is neither a cause nor effect on the persistence of Indian culture. But unique rights and a different culture are closely linked. While different cultures within Indian communities remain (and this seems likely through the foreseeable future), special rights of Indians will have to be recognized. The problem of granting these rights is a knotty and complex one, but it in no way lessens the need for granting them.

A first step toward a solution is to clarify the issues; it is hoped this report is a move in that direction. The heart of the matter is the unique position of Indians as a minority and the persistence of a distinct culture among Indians regardless of the pressures upon them. These two facets of the situation must be recognized in any proposals made for improving the civil rights of American Indians. The basis of most problems lies in the historic relationship between the federal government and the Indian tribes. The relation accounts for their special rights and in I.R.A. times contributed to cultural differences.

A beginning in any effort to extend civil rights is a simultaneous attack on poverty and the lack of self-government. Congressional leaders, such as former Senator Humphrey, and Bureau officials, such as Phileo Nash, have hinted at the approach, but, as pointed out previously, they seem preoccupied with economic conditions. If the war on poverty in reservation communities involves large expenditures and intensive planning, then the opportunity for Indians to learn responsibility for their own affairs is ideal. Of course, Indians must be convinced that important economic change is possible and they are the ones who must undertake it. Persuasion will be no easy matter because they have been long accustomed to rely on outside direction. Furthermore, they are aware of the many past shifts in Indian policy, and any change will first be seen as simply one more capricious act of the white man.

Assuming Indians can be convinced they will be responsible, a positive approach will require provision of necessary money for community services while giving up control over it. Policy should not be directed at saving money either to the detriment of Indians or in violation of treaty or moral obligations. Until reservations are developed economically, it will be necessary to finance from the outside. The process is likely to be a long one, but Indians must be assured of adequate economic aid.

Furthermore, a basic change is essential. Indian communities must be allowed to manage their own affairs, to administer their own social services in the same way as any other American community. As the undesirable results of outside management become more and more apparent, this approach should be obvious. Unfortunately, under termination policy of the 1950's, first thought was to transfer the Indian problem into the hands of the states. Such a transfer would have solved nothing; state governments would have become the paternalistic agent. If the Indian communities are to develop, both socially and economically, they must be given the power to manage their own affairs. Outside help in learning this management is not only desirable but essential; yet, the "help" must clearly be assistance in learning, not management itself which is presently the case. The argument has been advanced in clear terms by Sol Tax.[50]

> Congress does not like the idea of Indian communities being controlled by a government bureau. Neither do the Indians. At the same time, if Indians cannot pay for their own social services, someone has to – whether State or Federal governments. But why, if we want to get rid of the over-control of Indian communities, must we, also, cut off needed subsidies? In some manner the administration and the subsidy of Indian community services, like health and education, must be separated. Just as farmers who receive large subsidies from the federal government are still permitted to run their farms and make their own mistakes, so could it be with Indian communities. If then, finally, we (1) stop frightening Indians by threatening to dissolve the symbolic relationship so important in Indian eyes between the federal government and themselves; (2) continue federal subsidies where necessary; but (3) remove the traditional over-administration and control of Indian affairs (even if this takes drastic revision of federal Indian laws) and allow Indian communities to decide their own destinies, it seems to us certain that there will occur an Indian development and adjustment of a kind we have never seen. Should it surprise us that the right way turns out

**to be the way that fits American values of freedom and local-determination?**

The policy of developing true self-government, coupled with economic assistance, is at the heart of the "Indian problem." Of course, not all civil rights issues will be fully solved even if such policy is adopted eventually. Although the policy would likely make tribal jurisdiction clear and distinct, tribal courts need to be strengthened. Most law codes and tribal constitutions need revisions; in the process provisions for full civil rights guaranteed by the Constitution could be included. It may be necessary to allow for a transition from present systems to improved ones, but such a step is feasible. The greatest necessity is simply to recognize the need for new courtroom procedures and the fact that customs, such as due process, cannot be introduced immediately. Nor do the systems which eventually evolve have to be identical with neighboring white communities. Social control in any small community is going to vary at points from American ideals. Indian communities cannot be expected to achieve the ideal any better than people of Plainville or Homestead. Certainly, American ideals of toleration and appreciation of differences should allow Indians to evolve their own procedures and standards of justice with the frame of reference provided by the Constitution and applicable legislation. Likewise, special areas such as education and religion may require clarifying legislation and judicial review, but surely the American value of self-determination should allow Indian communities to differ from other Americans on these points. Congressional and state action will help in insuring rights to self-determination, but an interested, informed and sympathetic public also would be a major aid. The latter is a necessity not only to insure passage of appropriate legislation but also to reduce to a minimum still existing prejudices and discrimination which prevent Indians from achieving equality with other citizens.

# Chapter 9

# Bibliography

American Indian Chicago Conference
1961 "Declaration of Indian Purpose." Chicago.

Basehart, Harry and Sasaki, Tom
1964 "Changing Political Organization in the Jicarilla Apache Reservation Community." *Human Organization*, Vol. 24, No. 4.

Cohen, Felix S.
1960 *The Legal Conscience: Selected Papers of Felix S. Cohen.* New Haven: Yale University Press.

Farber, W.O., Odeen, Philip and Tschetter, Robert
1957 *Indians, Law Enforcement and Local Government.* Report No. 37, Vermillion, South Dakota: Governmental Research Bureau and Institute of Indian Studies.

Hadley, J. Nixon
1957 "The Demography of the American Indian." *The Annals of the American Academy of Political and Social Science*, Vol. 311.

Havinghurst, Robert and Neugarten, Bernice
1955 *American Indian and White Children.* Chicago: University of Chicago Press.

Havinghurst, Robert
1957 "Education Among American Indians: Individual and Cultural Aspects." *The Annals of the American Academy of Political and Social Science*, Vol. 311.

Joseph, Alice, Spicer, Rosamond and Chesky, Jane
1949 *The Desert People.* Chicago: University of Chicago Press.

La Barre, Weston, McAllester, David, Slotkin, J.S., Stewart, Omer and Tax, Sol
1951 "Statement of Peyote." *Science,* Vol. 114.

Leighton, Dorothea and Kluckhohn, Clyde
1947 *Children of the People.* Cambridge: Harvard University Press.

LaFarge, Oliver
1956 "To Be Free and Equal." *The American Indian,* Vol. 7, No. 3.

Longaker, Richard
1956 "Andrew Jackson and the Judiciary. Presidential Defiance: The Georgian Controversy." *Political Science Quarterly.* Vol. 71.

MacGregor, Gordon
1946 *Warriors Without Weapons.* Chicago: University of Chicago Press.

McNickle, D'Arcy
1957 "How to Help Indians Help Themselves." *American Indians* (ed.) Walter Daniels, New York: H. Wilson Co.

Meriam, Lewis
1928 *The Problems of Indian Administration.* Baltimore: Johns Hopkins Press.

Provinse, John, *et al.*
1954 "The American Indian in Transition." *American Anthropologist,* Vol. 56.

Report of the Task Force on Indian Affairs
1961 (mimeo.)

Shotwell, Louisa
1957 "Who Are the American Indians." *American Indian.* (ed.) Walter Daniels, New York: H. Wilson Co.

Slotkin, J.S.
1956 *The Peyote Religion: A Study in Indian-White Relations.* Glencoe: The Free Press

Tax, Sol
1956 "The Freedom to Make Mistakes." *America Indigena,* Vol. 16, No. 3.

Tax, Sol, Thomas, Robert and Stanley, Samuel
1957 "1950 Distribution of Descendants of the Aboriginal Population of Alaska, Canada and the United States." Chicago: Department of Antrhopology, University of Chicago.

Tax, Sol
1958 "A Positive Program for the Indian." *The American Indian*, Vol. 8, No. 1.

Thompson, Hildegard
1957 "Education Among American Indians: Institutional Aspects." *Annals of the American Academy of Political and Social Science*, Vol. 311.

Thompson, Laura and Joseph, Alice
1944 *The Hopi Way*. Chicago: University of Chicago Press.

Underhill, Ruth
1953 *Red Man's America*. Chicago: University of Chicago Press.

U.S. Senate
1929 "Hearings Before a Subcommittee on Indian Affairs." 71st Congress, 2nd Session. South Dakota, Part 7, July.

1962 "Constitutional Rights." Subcommittee on Constitutional Rights, Committee on the Judiciary, Report No. 1455, May.

1962 "Hearings Before the Subcommittee on Constitutional Rights." 87th Congress, 2nd Session. Part 3, June.

1963 "Constitutional Rights." Subcommittee on Constitutional Rights, Committee on the Judiciary, Report No. 164, April.

Vogt, Evon
1955 *Modern Homesteaders*. Cambridge: Harvard University Press.

Wax, Murray and Rosalie
1964 "Formal Education in an American Indian Community." *Supplement to Social Problems*, Vol. 11, No. 4.

West, James
1945 *Plainville, U.S.A.* New York: Columbia University Press.

# Addenda

Bean, L.J. and Wood, Corinne
1969 *The Crisis in Indian Health.* The Indian Historian, Vol. 2, No. 3, Fall.

Brophy, William and Aberle, Sophie D.
1966 *The Indian: America's Unfinished Business.* Norman: University of Oklahoma Press.

Costo, Rupert and Henry, Jeannette
1970 *Textbooks and the American Indian.* San Francisco: The Indian Historian Press.

Deloria, Vine Jr.
1969 *Custer Died for Your Sins.* New York: Macmillan.

Haas, Theodore H.
1957 *The Legal Aspects of Indian Affairs from 1887 to 1957,* in Simpson, George and Milton Yinger, editors: American Indians in American Life, Annals of the American Academy of Political and Social Science, 1957.

Hodge, William.
1969 *The Albuquerque Navajos.* University of Arizona Anthropological Papers II.

House Committee on Interior and Insular Affairs
1953, 1954 *Investigation of the Bureau of Indian Affairs.*

Indian Record
1969 *Economic Development,* special issue, October, Department of the Interior, U.S. Government Printing Office.

Jorgensen, Joseph G.
1970 *Indians and the Metropolis.*

Sub-Committee on Indian Education
1969 Hearings and Reports, with extensive bibliography.

Wagner, Carruth J. and Rabeau, Erwin S.
1964 *Indian Poverty and Indian Health.* Health, Education and Welfare Indicators, March.

See also, *The Navajo Times,* Window Rock, Arizona; *The Rosebud Sioux Herald,* Pine Ridge, South Dakota; all of 1969.

# References

1. Declaration of Indian Purpose. Report of the American Indian Chicago Conference, June, 1961, p. 15.

2. Ibid., p. 15.

3. Ibid., p. 16.

4. Quoted in ibid., p. 16.

5. Sandra Johnson. "The Indian Progress." Report of the 1964 Workshop on Indian Affairs. Quoted in: Institute of Indian Studies, News Report No. 21, November, 1964.

6. Felix Cohen. *The Legal Conscience: Selected Papers of Felix S. Cohen.* New Haven: Yale University Press, 1960, p. 255.

7. J. Nixon Hadley, "The Demography of the American Indians." *The Annals of the American Academy of Political and Social Science,* Vol. 311, May, 1957, pp. 23-30.

8. Sol Tax, Robert Thomas, Samuel Stanley, "1950 Distribution of Descendants of the Aboriginal Population of Alaska, Canada and the United States," Department of Anthropology, University of Chicago, 1957.

9. Louisa Shotwell, "Who Are the American Indians?" *American Indians,* ed. Walter Daniels; New York: H.W. Wilson Company, 1957, p. 11.

10. "Hearings Before a Subcommittee of the Committee on Indian Affairs, United States Senate, 71st Congress, 2nd Session," *South Dakota,* part 7, July, 1929, pp. 2827-28.

11. Ruth Underhill, *Red Man's America* (Chicago: University of Chicago Press, 1953), pp. 108-109.

12. Richard Longaker, "Andrew Jackson and the Judiciary. Presidential Defiance: The Georgian Controversy," *Political Science Quarterly,* Vol. 71 (September, 1956), pp. 343-50.

13. Ibid., p. 347.

14. Felix Cohen, "Indians Are Citizens," *The Legal Conscience: Selected Papers of Felix S. Cohen.* (New Haven: Yale University Press, 1960) p. 253.

15. Ibid., pp. 254-255.

16. "Hearings Before Subcommittee on Constitutional Rights Pursuant to Senate Resolution 260," Part 3 (Washington: U.S. Government Printing Office, 1963).

17. "Constitutional Rights." Report No. 1455 of the Committee on the Judiciary, U.S. Senate, Subcommittee on Constitutional Rights, May, 1962.

18. Ibid., p. 24.

19. "Constitutional Rights of the American Indians." Hearings Before the Subcommittee on Constitutional Rights of the Committee on the Judiciary, U.S. Senate, Part 4, March, 1963, pp. 872-3.

20. W.O. Farber, Philip Odeen, Robert Tschetter. *Indians, Law Enforcement and Local Government,* Report No. 37, Governmental Research Bureau and Institute of Indian Studies, Vermillion, South Dakota, 1957.

21. "Declaration of Indian Purpose," Report of the American Indian Chicago Conference, 1961, p. 13.

22. W.O. Farber et al., pp. 64-68.

23. "A Program for Indian Citizens," Report of the Fund for the Republic, 1961, p. 24.

24. Report of the Task Force on Indian Affairs, July, 1961, p. 30.

25. "Constitutional Rights," Report of the Subcommittee on Constitutional Rights. Report No. 164, April, 1963, p. 9.

26. Report of the Task Force on Indian Affairs, July, 1961, p. 22.

27. Murray and Rosalie Wax, Formal Education in an American Indian Community, *Supplement to Social Problems,* Vol. 11, No. 4, Spring, 1964.

28. Report of the Task Force on Indian Affairs, July, 1961, p. 25.

29. Ernest Schusky, "Missions and Government Policy in Dakota Indian Communities," *Practical Anthropology,* Vol. 10, No. 3, June, 1963.

30. State of Arizona vs. Mary Attakai, Superior Court, Coconino County, Arizona, July 26, 1960, No. 4098.

31. Ernest Schusky. Field Notes. Lower Brule, South Dakota, 1958.

32. James West. *Plainville, U.S.A.* New York: Columbia University Press, 1945, pp. 97-98.

33. Evon Vogt. *Modern Homesteaders.* Cambridge: Harvard University Press, 1955, pp. 155-60.

34. Evon Vogt. *Modern Homesteaders.* Cambridge: Harvard University Press, 1955, p. 158.

35. Ernest Schusky. Field Notes. Yankton, South Dakota, 1960.

36. Oliver LaFarge. "To Be Free and Equal." *The American Indian.* Vol. VII, No. 3, Spring, 1956, pp. 5-14.

37. Harry Basehart and Tom Sasaki. "Changing Political Organization in the Jicarilla Apache Reservation Community." *Human Organization,* Vol. 24, No. 4, 1964, p. 285.

38. Ibid., p. 289.

39. Sol Tax. "The Freedom to Make Mistakes." *America Indigena,* Vol. 16, No. 3, October, 1956.

40. Gordon MacGregor. *Warriors Without Weapons.* Chicago: University of Chicago Press, 1945; Alice Joseph, Rosamond Spicer and Jane Chesky. *The Desert People.* Chicago: University of Chicago Press, 1949; Dorothea Leighton and Clyde Kluckhohn. *Children of the People.* Cambridge: Harvard University Press, 1947; Laura Thompson and Alice Joseph. *The Hopi Way.* Chicago: University of Chicago Press, 1944; Robert Havinghurst and Bernice Neugarten. *American Indian and White Children.* Chicago: University of Chicago Press, 1955.

41. Hildegard Thompson. "Education Among American Indians: Institutional Aspects." *American Indians and American Life.* Annals of the American Academy of Political and Social Science. Vol. 311, May, 1957.

42. Robert Havinghurst. "Education Among American Indians: Individual and Cultural Aspects." Ibid.

43. Lewis Meriam. *The Problems of Indian Administration.* Baltimore: Johns Hopkins Press, 1928.

44. Hildegard Thompson. Op. cit., p. 101.

45. Murray and Rosalie Wax. Op. cit.

46. J.S. Slotkin. *The Peyote Religion: A Study in Indian-White Relations.* Glencoe: The Free Press, 1956, p. 50.

47. Weston LaBarre, David McAllester, J.S. Slotkin, Omer Stewart and Sol Tax. "Statement on Peyote." *Science,* Vol. 114, November, 1951, p. 582.

48. D'Arcy McNickle, "How to Help Indians Help Themselves." *American Indians,* (ed.) Walter Daniels, New York: H.H. Wilson Co., 1957, p. 188.

49. John Provinse *et al.* "The American Indian in Transition." *American Anthropologist,* Vol. 56, June, 1954, p. 388.

50. Sol Tax, "A Positive Program for the Indian," *The American Indian.* Vol. 8, No. 1, Spring, 1958, p. 9-10.